THE FUTURE

OF

INSURANCE

From Disruption to Evolution

Volume IV. Asia Rising

Blazing New Paths in the Asian Insurance Market

THERESA BLISSING
WITH BRYAN FALCHUK

Insurance Evolution Press 📖

Published by Insurance Evolution Press
Boston, Massachusetts
Copyright © 2023 Insurance Evolution Partners

DEDICATION

To my parents, who first opened the world to me and planted the seeds of curiosity in my heart.

CONTENTS

FOREWORD FROM WALTER DE OUDE

Insurance is not an exciting business. It's just something that everyone needs. It's pretty boring most of the time. Most insurers have struggled to find a way to bridge the gap between delivering a product that is new and exciting and welcoming, and a product that we have to hard sell to get people to buy.

Insurance is also an industry steeped in tradition and age-old practices. It has often lagged behind other industries in today's world of rapid technological change, as witnessed in other financial sectors. Where innovation in payment methods, cross-border transactions, and modern banking flourished with cutting-edge new ideas, the insurance world has been stubbornly reluctant to turn the page on how it works. Whether because of complexity, inertia, bureaucracy or legacy, innovation has not been our key attribute. However, the last few years have definitely been a wakeup call, indicating an evident shift.

The story of Singlife aptly encapsulates this transformation.

When I started Singlife, I saw two major opportunities in the life insurance space. First was the lack of an awesome direct customer experience, slow processes, and too much paperwork in our space. This all suggested that there was a big opportunity to digitize the mechanics of the insurance offering and delight people with the experience. This transition could pave the way for a new distribution approach, a new marketplace and a new way of engaging with customers. Ultimately, this was about giving a fresh face to insurance – one that makes you happy when you think about it, rather than the "grudge purchase" it has historically been known as.

The second opportunity that stood out in Singapore was its reputation as Asia's wealth hub. With Singapore witnessing substantial foreign capital influx at the time, it was an opportune moment for Singlife. During our inception, prevailing interest rates made products like universal life particularly appealing. With private banking exploring new revenue streams, universal life products became highly sought after. Singlife strategically positioned itself to capitalize on this trend at that particular point in time.

Singapore, renowned for its well-regulated and secure financial services ecosystems, offered an ideal base for such an ambitious endeavour. Singapore had not had a new life insurance company in over 40 years. While many questioned the choice due to the country's rigorous regulations, I saw them as a strength. To me, these challenges were an opportunity to establish credibility and stability for a new type of insurer. I believe in aiming for the gold standard; if you can succeed in Singapore, you can be successful anywhere.

Establishing a fresh Life insurance company from the ground up was not a simple task, and not just due to the need to raise capital and prove the viability of the business. Starting with nothing more than an empty canvas was daunting. Writing the initial line of code or blueprint can take immense planning, as it sets the foundation upon which all else is built.

During Singlife's early days, our initial hurdle was to raise capital. To assure the Monetary Authority of Singapore of our venture's solidity, we embarked on a challenging endeavor to raise SG$50 million. It was not the easiest job in the world, but we had massive support from our early investors and managed to raise the funds within three years.

During that initial period from inception to securing funding, our primary focus was on developing innovative technology. While capital-raising efforts ran concurrently, our passion for crafting cutting-edge tech remained at the forefront. We identified glaring inefficiencies in traditional policy issuance, underwriting and administration. It felt thrilling to lead the digital shift for the industry here. It was a massive opportunity to capitalize on while the rest of the insurance sector lagged, with its heavy reliance on dated, paper-based processes and lack of the technology for instant policy issuance or automated know-your-customer (KYC) and anti-money-laundering (AML) checks.

At the time, everything in the insurance industry in Singapore was done by paper, nothing was digital. Our ambition was to digitize, make the insurance journey as human-free as possible and transform the industry into something more accessible, inviting, and engaging, and in doing so, create a new marketplace.

By 2017, with licenses secured, Singlife was primed for its grand unveiling as Singapore's first new digital Life insurer and the first insurer to be granted an underwriting license in four decades.

The new brand was very well received in the market. Our innovative digital approach resonated with a tech-savvy demographic, fueling explosive initial growth. Yet, with time, we recognized the limitations of focusing solely on the digitally-native population.

We saw the need to pivot our strategy, leveraging our direct digital capabilities to offer immediate access to financial advisors. This enabled them to engage with their clients in a far more efficient manner, utilizing our technology to expedite policy issuance and streamline their sales process. Insurance could be sold by an adviser in one sitting with the customer, rather than the traditional approach where iterations of interactions were the norm. This strategic shift significantly boosted our growth once again, propelling our business forward.

As we progressed, we consistently refined our technology and processes, always with a digital-first approach at the core. Our teams were lean and efficient, minimizing bureaucracy and emphasizing streamlined workflows. We were Sparta vs. the Syrians – warriors in a war against the old and the slow.

We were also fortunate to witness certain market shifts, one of which presented us with the golden chance to acquire Zurich's operations in Singapore. Zurich had strategically chosen to withdraw from the Singaporean market, seeking buyers for their existing ventures. For us, this was a fantastic opportunity, especially considering the notable similarities between our product offerings and Zurich's established portfolio.

Incorporating Zurich's operations into the Singlife framework, bolstered by our innovative technologies, marked a monumental advancement for us. Our proprietary platform ensured that the integration was smooth and efficient, unparalleled to any I had experienced before – even in my tenure with industry giants like HSBC. Our technological edge in the acquisition was evident in our ability to transition everything to our custom-built systems swiftly and effectively. We avoided prolonged transitional phases and executed the acquisition seamlessly.

My point here is that today's innovation lays the groundwork for future advantages. This foresight becomes valuable in various scenarios, from adapting to business shifts and facilitating acquisitions to pivoting and altering business strategies.

> *"...today's innovation lays the groundwork for future advantages."*
>
> – Walter de Oude, Founder, Singlife

The next major milestone for Singlife was the delivery of a product called the Singlife Account. I found myself pondering, "Why should banks be the exclusive custodians of customer cash relationships? If an insurer could cultivate these cash relationships, they could potentially guide them into more sophisticated, high-value insurance products."

With this vision, we launched the Singlife Account. Its primary offering was a 2.5% return on deposits, capped at SG$10,000 – a significant leap from the 50 basis points banks were offering at the time.

The response was overwhelming. In a mere seven months, we collected over SG$1 billion and welcomed over 100,000 customers onto our platform.

Yet, the brilliance of this innovation wasn't merely the product itself. It symbolized a groundbreaking shift, granting a life insurance company access to a realm once exclusively reserved for banks. The Singlife Account was more than just an account; it was a doorway into the expansive financial services landscape. By offering an enticing alternative to traditional bank deposits, Singlife positioned itself to compete directly with banks, delivering greater potential returns for customers.

However, this wasn't simply a game of product outpacing. The Singlife Account represented a paradigm shift, underlining our intent to serve customers across multiple financial dimensions. We recognized that life insurance can be a challenging sell, with many postponing the essential decision to secure their futures. However, by engaging customers through their immediate cash needs, we found a channel to usher them into higher-value products, spanning investments, long-term savings, health and critical illness plans, and ultimately, the crown jewel of insurance offerings: Term Life insurance.

By encompassing this broad spectrum, Singlife moved beyond traditional boundaries, fostering profound and lasting relationships with clients. We offered an alternative not just to bank products, but to conventional banking experiences altogether.

I firmly believe that the most innovative thing that the life insurance industry has seen in the last few years was Singlife's development and launch of the Singlife Account.

My vision for the Singlife Account was to position it as the gateway to the world of insurance. I envisioned a streamlined, digital onboarding process that would foster a cash-like relationship, establishing it as the core around which all personal financial engagements revolved. This product, to me, symbolized an untapped goldmine in the financial services sphere – an unprecedented innovation. It marked an opportunity for Singlife not only to stand out as a pioneering digital force but also to deliver genuine, tangible benefits to our clients.

Of course, this is an incredibly complicated thing to do and it necessitated Singlife to operate outside of its comfort zone. The endeavor required additional licensing, which was granted by the Monetary Authority of Singapore, allowing Singlife to extend its offering to payment services.

It also demanded extensive groundwork. We had to lay bank-equivalent foundations, develop payment proficiencies, and shoulder the substantial compliance demands related to transaction monitoring, AML, and more. The magnitude of the undertaking was immense.

Yet, the potential advantages of this undertaking were equally monumental. Incorporating debit cards and a payment infrastructure expanded our scope, paving the way for comprehensive wealth management. Just consider the transformative effects on health insurance: handling the nuances of deductibles or co-payments through a unified platform, making the claims process more fluid, and expediting the disbursement of claim funds — all under the seamless umbrella of Singlife's ecosystem.

In 2019, Singlife's story took another turn. UK insurer Aviva shifted its focus back to its domestic markets, contemplating an exit from Singapore. For me, this signaled another golden opportunity to further elevate Singlife's already remarkable trajectory by incorporating Aviva's capabilities and resources into Singlife.

Singlife had already seen phenomenal growth, powered by its technological advances and innovative financial product strategies. I believed that by melding Aviva's expertise into the Singlife framework, our route to sector dominance could be exponentially fast-tracked.

Aviva was not just any company; it was a profitable venture with strong cash flows, vital for nurturing growth. Moreover, their expansive customer base of 1.5 million presented an immediate opportunity to leverage Singlife's cash-centric, transactional capabilities. Aviva's diverse product suite, encompassing Health insurance, General insurance, and niche offerings like Elder Care, would enrich our portfolio. Integrating these into Singlife's platform promised to significantly amplify our customer engagement and operational breadth.

I sought to execute that transaction with vigor and unmatched determination. This led to new thinking on how innovative startups can structure deals. We identified a way that allowed us to venture into arenas of acquisitions, mergers, and more complex financial engineering.

In our arrangement, we valued Singlife at approximately SG$500 million (~US$370 million) and Aviva's business at SG$2.7 billion (~US$2.0 billion). Businesses cannot normally acquire someone five times larger, so this deal would require new thinking to make it happen. We constructed a mechanism whereby the SG$3.2 billion combined entity would be financed in part with bank debt, a bond issuance and some structured finance, together with private equity capital and additional capital from our shareholders, Sumitomo, at the time. This approach showcased a novel method in capital management, structure, and regulatory compliance, aiming for a seamless and financially efficient merger. I took immense pride in orchestrating such a groundbreaking transaction. The merger of Singlife and Aviva Singapore marked the most significant insurance transaction ever in Singapore's history.

However, not all of Singlife's new investor stakeholders at that time echoed my strategic aspirations for the heights we might reach. The stable, dependable value creation of more traditional tried and tested distribution models seemed a golden goose too precious to risk with internal disruption.

So as it turned out, in the end my personal vision for Singlife differed somewhat from that of its new stakeholders. While I passionately championed cash and cash-like solutions as the cornerstone of our customer relationships, this direction wasn't where the new, combined entity was destined to go. Ultimately, this led to a parting of ways.

I've always loved Singlife. I've loved everything that we built there, and I've loved the innovation that we had brought to bear. Singlife will always be part of my DNA, and I will always support its business. But as the sands of time shift, so must we.

As I embark on a fresh chapter, my appetite for innovation remains undiminished. My next business is called Chocolate Finance, aiming to pick up where my version of Singlife left off – focusing on innovations in the cash management arena, particularly in card payments and transactions. However, this time, the lens isn't solely insurance but asset management, where I foresee the next wave of groundbreaking innovation taking place.

Having been a bystander of innovation in the insurance sector over the last 20 years of my life, and being fortunate enough to have played a meaningful role in the evolution of the industry, I look back at everything that has happened around me as the industry has transformed itself. I'm proud of the contribution that Singlife made to the industry as a whole and I'm absolutely sure it will continue to innovate in its own way, going forward.

The lessons I've derived from Singlife's trajectory hold profound significance for me. But beyond my personal reflections, Singlife's story serves as a testament to the boundless possibilities that lie ahead for the industry. To those who have tracked our path, and even those just becoming familiar, there's much to glean. In this era of rapid transformation, the mandate is clear: innovate, adapt, learn, and pivot.

Today's global insurance landscape is not just about hedging against uncertainties; it's about crafting value-rich experiences for customers. It's about leveraging technology to provide solutions that are not just transactional, but deeply engaging and impactful. It's not just about insurance innovation – it's the whole financial services landscape that's up for grabs.

There is a vast canvas of opportunity awaiting those who dare to reimagine the realm of insurance. These opportunities, driven by shifting market trends, invite insurance firms to rise to the occasion and design innovative, engaging, and economically sound solutions that align with contemporary consumer preferences.

This entry in *The Future of Insurance* series is more than just a chronicle of past milestones or current trends. It's a visionary dive into the numerous innovative endeavors unfolding across Asia and globally. While Singlife's story is just a fragment, I hope it exemplifies the spirit of transformation and innovation that this book aims to capture.

As you delve deeper into these pages and the different case studies featured in this book, I hope you find not just information but inspiration. Herein lies a treasure trove of insights, anecdotes, and forward-looking perspectives that, I believe, will enrich your understanding and spark your imagination for what lies ahead in the world of insurance.

Wishing you an enlightening journey through *The Future of Insurance, Volume IV. Asia Rising*.

– Walter De Oude
Founder, Singlife

PREFACE

Writing a book about innovation and the future of insurance is a race against time. Never before in history has transformation occurred at such a rapid pace. COVID-19 has further accelerated the digital transformation of insurance and forced even the most conservative players in the market to invest in the digitization of their business.

In an ever-changing world, my aim for this book is to identify universal concepts that are used by some of the most innovative companies in the insurance space. I want to share how these organizations, small and large, are pushing the boundaries and designing the future of our industry.
This book is not centered solely on established insurance incumbents or on insurtech startups. Instead, it is focused on how companies in different parts of Asia are defining their own future of insurance and how this can look, at least in part, very different to what we have witnessed in Western countries.

Let me explain why with a metaphor. My parents are the proud owners of a centuries-old, half-timbered house in the Frankfurt area of Germany. This house, constructed in 1652, is an architectural marvel. Its walls have withstood the test of time for centuries.

However, every time my parents plan even minor renovations, they must navigate a maze of regulations, due to strict German heritage conservation laws and technical constraints given the home's age to ensure that they do not damage the integrity of the structure.

Purchasing building materials off the shelf often becomes a challenge as numerous walls are irregular, windows lack perfect right angles, and much of the plumbing and electrical wiring dates back to the dawn of electrical power.

I hope you see the similarities between renovating an old house and implementing insurance innovation. The insurance industry has been around for centuries, and it has undergone significant changes over time. However, as in the case of an old house, implementing these changes is not without challenges. There are many obstacles to overcome, including regulatory hurdles, technological constraints, and resistance to change from within the industry.

An advantage in parts of developing Asia is the fact that they do not have centuries-old legacy systems to contend with. New players can often start on a green field, or at least with fewer constraints than they might face in a more developed environment. This makes the adoption of new technologies much faster and can allow for the leapfrogging of certain development stages.

Let me give you another example. I grew up during the time when the internet first became available for individual households. The first time I accessed the internet was through a personal computer connecting via our telephone land line. However, in parts of developing Asia, the first time many people accessed the internet was through a smartphone.

In 2010, only 100 million people in India – less than 10% of the population – had access to the internet. Ten years later, 465 million were online thanks to their smartphones.[1]

The impact of how people first started using the internet can still be felt today across the world.

In May 2023, the internet traffic share in the USA was 60.1% through mobile and tablets, and 39.9% through desktop and laptop computers. During the same period in India, on the other hand, we saw 81.4% of traffic come through mobile and tablets and only 18.6% through desktop and laptop computers.[2] This has an immense impact on how products and services are marketed and consumed online. India has developed a mobile-first strategy and leading organizations

---

[1] "Why India's Smartphone Revolution Is a Double-edged Sword," *Knowledge at Wharton*, 11 May 2023.
[2] "Mobile vs. Desktop vs. Tablet Traffic Market Share," Similarweb, as of 20 June 2023.

consequentially prioritize investments in their mobile customer journey over the computer experience.

This goes beyond the actions of companies and consumers alone. The Indian government and others also factor in the significance of mobile devices when making decisions on matters such as regulations, transportation, and more, as we will see in some of the stories in this book.

This is just one of the reasons why I believe some of the companies we find in Asia are leading in certain areas when it comes to innovation and the adoption of new technologies. However, it is impossible and naïve to generalize across all of Asia. A continent so large and diverse, not only in terms of culture and religion, but also in terms of economic development stages, cannot be looked at homogenously or uniformly.

Depending on who you ask, China is close to overtaking the US in terms of economic power and is among the world leaders in telecommunication technology and artificial intelligence (AI). When it comes to insurance penetration, China has outpaced the US, proclaiming an insurance premium that accounts for 20.5% of its GDP, compared to the US's 12.4% in 2021. In stark contrast, countries like Indonesia register a mere 1.6% insurance penetration.[3] This indicates significant growth potential, especially when considering that Indonesia, with its population exceeding 270 million, has one of the fastest growing middle classes in Southeast Asia.

In this book, I will not be able to cover all the great innovations that are happening in this part of the world. But I hope to give a glimpse of some of the amazing stories of how different insurance players are shaping the future of insurance in their country.

This book is not only for those who are interested in what is happening in Asia. It aims to discover some universal truths and lessons that apply to any organization wanting to innovate. It also aims to be an inspiration for organizations around the globe and might give an indication of what types of developments we can expect in other regions.

---

[3] Insurance indicators: Penetration, OECD Stat, as of 10 August 2023.

I. PRE-HISTORY

Life is a series of choices and opportunities, and it is through these moments that we define our path and shape our future. As I write this chapter, I am reminded of the countless choices I have made throughout my life that have led me to this very moment. Specifically, the choice to connect with Bryan Falchuk, without whom this book probably never would have existed in the first place.

So, why did I feel like I had to write this book when Bryan approached me with this opportunity? Over the years, I have had the privilege of working with remarkable individuals and organizations, witnessing firsthand their triumphs and successes.

This book is about some of those outstanding people and organizations that are shaping the future of insurance in Asia and beyond. I am grateful to each and every one of them for sharing their experiences, insights, and lessons learned to help the industry as a whole navigate the challenges and seize the opportunities that lie ahead.

Before we dive into their stories, please allow me to tell you a little bit about myself, how I got here and why, as a German citizen living in New York, I decided to write a book on the Asian insurance market.

When you ask people who have worked their entire lives in insurance about how they ended up in this field, the majority will give you one of the following two answers: by accident or because a family member was working in insurance. For me it was the latter.

My parents owned an insurance agency and ran it together for over 40 years. Their office was on the first floor of my childhood home and therefore insurance was inevitably all around me from the day I was born. I remember countless evenings where my parents discussed their work and the challenges they faced over dinner.

Looking back, this was not a very healthy work-life balance but, somehow, I still decided to pursue a career in insurance. In August 2004, I joined Italian insurer Generali in their Corporate Life division in Frankfurt, Germany. I started as a key account manager but quickly got involved with different local and international projects.

In 2007, I got the opportunity to work on a major merger between the German branch of Generali and German insurer Volksfürsorge. Both organizations already belonged to the Generali group and were equal in size, with both serving Life and P&C. Being part of the global Generali group, the brand name of the newly merged entity was obviously going to be Generali but everything else was essentially up for grabs, ideally taking the best out of both worlds into the new entity.

I was part of the team that was to design the future of the Corporate Life division. Both organizations had a strong Corporate Life portfolio, however the product strategies of the two companies were slightly different and so was the technology they deployed. I learned a lot during this time, including how messy things can get when emotions are high. There was a large amount of uncertainty, and people across all different levels were wondering if their skills were still needed in the newly merged company, and, consequently, if they would still have a job. We came to the realization that it was not the time to completely shake things up but to find a compromise.

A couple of years later, however, we realized that the structure we had designed during the merger did not work and we were not getting the market traction we had hoped for. Thus, we launched a new project to define a new business model for the division. I was assigned to lead the project to implement the new business processes, manage the necessary portfolio migrations and oversee the entire change management process.

While in previous projects I had already witnessed the constraints of legacy systems and the costs of migrating life insurance portfolios, this time I experienced first-hand the challenges around changing people's behavior.

While the other challenges could theoretically be solved by throwing money at the problem, or IT person-days for that matter, working with people and trying to convince them to embrace the changes is a totally different story. It is an often overlooked or low-priority challenge, but I came to understand that changing people's behavior and mindset is probably the most difficult challenge to solve and maybe the most important. Afterall, whether you succeed or fail heavily depends on people buying into your vision and their willingness to follow you into this new world.

While I did value the opportunities to work on those strategic projects designing the future of the new corporate life division, what really excited me was my time with Generali in Hong Kong. In 2009, I moved to Hong Kong for the first time and was working at the regional head office. This was part of a career development program and I worked with a number of different divisions.

It was during this time that Generali launched some of their Asian local insurers like Generali Indonesia or Future Generali in India. I was amazed how different their challenges were and how tirelessly the teams worked on building these new insurers in Asia. The mindset and corporate culture were unlike what I had experienced in Germany, and it left me inspired.

I worked for the Generali group for over 10 years and held a range of different positions. In 2015, I was the Head of the International Employee Benefit Business for the German market but found myself missing the vibrant insurance landscape in Asia. I decided it was time for a change and made the move to take on a new challenge.

At Generali, I had always looked at ways technology can be used to help people work smarter and minimize human errors. When the term 'Big Data' gained popularity in the insurance industry, I was naturally curious about the impact. At the 2015 Insurance Government Leadership Network conference in London, Henri de Castries, previous Chairman and CEO of AXA Insurance, stated that big data "changes everything. It's the equivalent to oil and electricity a century ago and printing five or six centuries ago." I was intrigued and decided I wanted to learn more.

I understood the power of big data, however I also knew from my experience how siloed the data within an insurance carrier was and the difficulties around adopting new ways of working, especially if there is fear of becoming redundant. While there has been extensive research on the technical aspects of big data, there was a gap in peer-reviewed literature, suggesting a lack of research on adoption and the organizational changes it causes.

I decided to take a break from work life and accepted a scholarship for a master's program with American Webster University at their campus in Bangkok, Thailand. This gave me the opportunity to focus on a whole range of topics I had wanted to explore for a while, but never had the time to do.

At Webster, I conducted the first academic research study on the adoption of big data in the Southeast Asian insurance industry. I interviewed 28 insurance industry experts (mostly C-level insurance company executives) across Southeast Asia and Hong Kong. The research study's findings indicated big data implementation is not just a technological issue or a topic for information technology departments, as had been commonly perceived.

Challenges around the right IT infrastructure and access to credible and large enough data sets are widely discussed, but topics that are often overlooked are internal, organizational requirements. My research found that there is a need for organizational change in structure, culture, skills, and leadership.

In 2017, my professor Dr. Judith McIntyre and I published a paper based on my research and presented it at the International Conference on Business, Big-Data, and Decision Sciences (ICBBD).

To this day, I highly value this experience and can only recommend taking the time to go back into academia. Going back to university after a solid 10-year career run isn't just stepping back into the classroom, it's stepping forward into a whole new world of growth.

When you've been in the field, you get a lot of real-life, practical experiences under your belt. You've been problem-solving and doing the daily grind. That teaches you skills a textbook never could. Now, you take all that hands-on knowledge back to university, and guess what? You're not just learning, you're connecting dots, piecing together theory and practice in ways you never could have before.

On top of that, it was a chance for me to shake things up. I decided not to go back working for an insurance carrier but instead switched my career to management consulting. At first, I worked for German consulting firm Detecon before starting my own consulting and research practice, Accelerating Insurance. This gave me the freedom to work on projects I really enjoyed while getting to continue my research on innovation topics.

In 2018, I started to dive deep into the InsurTech world. I worked with a number of startups and startup accelerators as well as with venture builder Whatnot on the concept of startup-as-a-service as a strategy for incumbent insurers to innovate.

I also continued working with universities and taught an undergraduate course at the Bangkok School of Management and was a guest lecturer at Chulalongkorn University and the Singapore College of Insurance. Another great experience that showed me the importance of connecting with younger generations to understand their priorities and what drives them.

During that time, I could feel that the perception of insurance was changing. When I started my career, insurance was perceived as a stable job with good career opportunities, but it was not something people got excited about. However, when talking about the importance of insurance for the overall economy and how technology can be deployed in so many new ways within insurance, my students suddenly became excited about the prospect of having a career in insurance.

I believe everyone in the industry started to feel this change. Insurance was suddenly sexy and even insurance regulators approached me to help them understand how InsurTech can be used to innovate the industry and make it more attractive for new talent.

I realized that while there was a lot of hype around InsurTech in the West, there was very limited information available on what was happening in Asia.

Rather than simply mirroring what was developing in the West, Asia needed its own solutions. Insurers in developing countries like India, for example, face very different challenges than companies in a mature market like the US. Consequentially I witnessed a range of Asian-born insurtechs emerge, ready to address the challenges in their country or region.

However, those developments were still widely ignored by the global insurance media. So, when I met Michael Waitze, who was running several Asia-focused tech podcasts out of Bangkok, we decided to start the Asia InsurTech Podcast.

We launched in May 2019, with the goal to give Asian InsurTech entrepreneurs, thought leaders, insurance executives and investors a platform to present and discuss how technology is helping reshape the Insurance industry in Asia. We were the first media company to bring Asia's success stories to a global audience and help the global InsurTech community understand key developments in this Region. In 2023, we are one of the largest InsurTech podcasts globally with listeners in over 150 countries.

Running the content side of the Asia InsurTech Podcast allowed me to connect with thought leaders globally, including Bryan Falchuk. We collaborated on a few podcasts together and, when Bryan approached me with the idea of writing a book on the Asian insurance market I did not hesitate.

However, turning this idea into reality took a bit longer than expected. Life has a way of getting in the way! So, after two long-distance moves, first to Sydney, Australia, then to New York City, finally here we are.

As we venture forth together to explore some of the Asian success stories, I encourage you to approach this journey with an open mind, a hunger for knowledge, and a willingness to embrace new perspectives. Remember, success is not a destination but a continuous process of learning, adapting, and evolving.

It is my sincerest hope that, by the end of this book, you will feel inspired to conquer the ever-evolving insurance landscape and are excited to be working in this field.

1. Embracing Innovation

During my career I have repeatedly experienced the numerous challenges that are linked to changing a person's mindset and their behavior. Humans are creatures of habit, meaning that entrenched behaviors are often difficult to shift due to the comfort found in the familiar. Additionally, cognitive biases such as confirmation bias and *status quo* bias can lead to resistance to change as people often seek out information that confirms their existing beliefs and tend to prefer maintaining the current state of affairs.

However, in our dynamic world, change is the only constant, an engine that propels our individual and collective evolution forward. It is through change that we grow, learn, adapt, and, ultimately, innovate. Change challenges our perspectives, disrupts our comfort zones, and compels us to question the *status quo*, fostering critical thinking and promoting creativity. Without change, we would remain stagnant and our potential untapped. Embracing change is an imperative not just for personal development but also for societal progress.

The question is, how can we enable people to embrace change and therefore innovation. During my research on the adoption of big data, I came across the diffusion of innovation theory developed by Everett Rogers, a renowned sociologist and communication scholar.[4] This theory seeks to explain how new ideas, technologies, products, or practices spread and are adopted by individuals and communities over time.

According to Rogers, the diffusion process occurs in five stages:

---

[4] Rogers, E., Everett M., *Diffusion of Innovations*. Free Press of Glencoe, New York, 1962.

1. Knowledge: This stage involves the introduction of an innovation to individuals or a community. People become aware of the innovation's existence, but they may have limited information about its benefits or how it works.

2. Persuasion: In this stage, individuals seek more information and evaluate the innovation. They weigh the advantages and disadvantages, considering factors like compatibility with their values, needs, and existing behaviors. They may also seek opinions from others or rely on influential figures for guidance.

3. Decision: At this point, individuals make a decision about whether to adopt or reject the innovation. This decision is influenced by various factors, including the perceived benefits, perceived risks, social norms, and personal circumstances.

4. Implementation: If individuals decide to adopt the innovation, they move into the implementation stage. They begin to use the innovation and integrate it into their daily lives or work routines. During this stage, individuals may face challenges or difficulties in adopting and adjusting to the new innovation.

5. Confirmation: In the final stage, individuals assess the results and outcomes of adopting the innovation. They evaluate whether the innovation meets their expectations, solves their problems, or delivers the promised benefits. Positive confirmation leads to reinforcement and continued use, while negative experiences may lead to discontinuation or rejection.

The diffusion of innovation theory also examines the rate or speed of adoption. Rogers found that the adoption of an innovation heavily depends on the decisions of other members of the same social system and the communication of the innovation. After about 10-25% of the members of a social system have adopted an innovation, the so-called innovators and early adopters, a tipping point is reached, and the majority will follow as kind of a domino effect. However, there are always laggards that are skeptical of an innovation and might never be convinced.

What was fascinating to observe was how the COVID-19 pandemic has, at least to a degree, accelerated the digital transformation of insurance. This was a completely different scenario that skipped some of the stages of Rogers' theory and showed how people abandon previous norms and beliefs when facing an existential threat. Suddenly, things were possible that many believed to be impossible prior to the pandemic.

For example, I still remember the countless discussions during my time at Generali about the possibility of working from home. It was a common request, especially from working mothers. Mainly technical constraints were brought forward as the primary reason this could not be offered. However, COVID-19 has proven that technology constraints were something most insurers could overcome within weeks. This is a reminder that barriers are often only in our heads and our norms rather than an immovable obstacle.

While many organizations have made some progress in their digitization strategy during the COVID-19 years, in many cases this was more of a catch-up period than a time of genuine innovation. However, I believe it was a wake-up call that organizations must become more digital in order to maintain their market position.

I also hope it will lead to more confidence in pursuing innovative ideas. Even without the force of a global pandemic, organizations can change and embrace innovation.

First with the Asia InsurTech Podcast and now with this book, I aim to introduce tech enthusiasts and visionaries working in insurance to innovations happening in the industry. After all, knowledge and persuasion are the first two stages of adopting an innovation, and if we can only inspire enough people, innovation will thrive in the insurance industry.

2. Blurred Lines

When I conducted interviews for my research study on the adoption of big data in the Southeast Asian Insurance industry, many of the experts I interviewed believed that the new technology will bring disruption to the industry.

One of the C-level executives I interviewed said, "I think it's a matter of time before Google and Amazon, who already hold banking and insurance licenses, are going to realize they can take the information they have and translate that data into concrete commercialization. That's going to be a wakeup call and it's going to wipe out the insurance companies."

This was in 2016, and, while Amazon has started selling insurance in India and the UK, we have not seen any major changes or disruption caused by tech players in the industry.

When the term InsurTech first gained popularity and startups like Lemonade and Metromile dominated the insurance news headlines, some again expected a disruption of the industry.

The reality is, we have not seen a major disruption caused by technology or the rise of InsurTech. What we have witnessed, however, was a wakeup call to the Insurance industry more broadly. Maybe this was accelerated by the fear of being disrupted or the impact of COVID-19, but I think it was also due to the vision those new insurtechs had which inspired many working in insurance.

Today, the lines between traditional insurance and InsurTech are blurred. It surely isn't insurtech startups against insurance incumbents or *vice versa*. Instead, we are seeing an ecosystem where players, young and old, come together to leverage each other's strengths to build the future of insurance.

While we do find a few insurtechs that call themselves disruptors and are trying to take on the well-established insurers, most insurtechs are looking for partnerships with insurers in a business-to-business (B2B) or business-to-business-to-consumer (B2B2C) model.

Many insurers have started to embrace InsurTech and are actively seeking partnerships to help their innovation journey. Global insurers are heavily investing in InsurTech and some are even founding their own startups.

Singapore insurtech bolttech was only launched in 2020. The company quickly gained traction globally and, in May 2023, announced it had raised US$196 million in Series B funding at a valuation of US$1.6 billion.[5] The latest funding round was let by Tokio Marine and MetLife and is a great example of the trust those global players have in the power of insurtech and the belief that collaboration will bring them forward.

The story of bolttech isn't that of a newcomer breaking into the insurtech sector on a shoestring budget. Instead, it's about a well-funded venture steered by seasoned industry professionals who, in part through strategic acquisitions, rapidly secured a global foothold.

Insurtechs like bolttech show that it is not necessarily industry outsiders and tech people that bring change to the industry. Instead, we see a story of opportunity for industry veterans with a vision to start up on a greenfield driving change in insurance.

The question is, how long do we call a company an insurtech? Despite their size and maturity as a business today, I believe most would argue that bolttech is an insurtech, but other examples are not as clear cut and raise the question of whether one's insurtech status can expire.

Let me explain what I mean with an example.

In 2017, Singlife was the first life insurer in Singapore to get granted a license since the 1970s. In 2018, the insurer acquired the business portfolio of Zurich Life and, in 2020, it acquired Aviva Singapore. The merger was the largest insurance deal in Singapore's history.[6]

Given that the company was only founded in 2017 as a digital-first insurer, many classify it as an insurtech, or maybe a neo-insurer.

---

[5] Wang, Catherine, "Billionaire Richard Li-backed Singapore Insurtech Unicorn raises $196 million," *Forbes*, 21 May 2023
[6] "About Us," Singlife, as of 21 May 2023

However, with the acquisition of Zurich Life and later Aviva Singapore, has Singlife reached incumbent status? Afterall, its underlying book of business primarily came from taking over legacy insurers in the country.

I believe the term insurtech shouldn't be reserved only for startups. For me, insurtech is the innovative intersection of insurance and technology. The way those companies are redefining how insurance products are designed, underwritten, and delivered and how they are helping incumbents work smarter and faster, and to innovate along the insurance value chain.

Insurance incumbents have understood the power of insurtech and many have adopted their own strategy to benefit from this wave of innovation in the industry.

Incumbent insurer Ping An is a great example of a company that has integrated insurtech into their overall corporate strategy. Ping An only operates as a licensed insurer in mainland China but is very active in the global startup space with its Global Voyager Fund. Through its strategic investment in a US startup, Ping An is arguably working in the disguise of an American insurtech with some of the largest insurers in the USA. We go deeper into this story in the chapter about Ping An.

The point I would like to make is that today, the traditional and insurtech parts of the Insurance industry are so intertwined that it's sometimes difficult to differentiate between the two. Arguably, all companies I discuss in this book can be considered an insurtech or have at least an insurtech component to them. I believe we shouldn't get caught up with labels but instead focus on how those companies are defining their future of insurance.

3. Asia Rising

As the most populous and culturally diverse continent, Asia's transformation into a powerhouse of global economics and technology is an example of human progress, resilience, and the willingness to embrace change. This Asian renaissance, largely driven by innovative technologies, population growth, economic liberalization, and increasing intra-regional connectivity, is redefining the world order. Some even argue it is shifting the axis of global power eastwards.

For the Insurance industry, Asia's rise presents both remarkable opportunities and profound challenges. The growing middle class, rising urbanization, and an ever-growing digital economy have created a vibrant and diverse market for insurance products and services. A large segment of the population in developing Asia is coming into the realm of insurability, fostering an immense, untapped market potential. Meanwhile, the rapid digitization trend is revolutionizing how insurance products are distributed and consumed, fostering a shift towards personalized, digitally enabled insurance services.

However, this rapid growth isn't without its trials. The industry must grapple with complex issues such as diverse regulatory environments, low levels of insurance awareness, evolving risk landscapes due to changes in consumer behavior as well as climate change and other macro factors. Adapting to these changing dynamics will determine who thrives and who falls behind.

Asia's vast diversity in terms of cultures, languages, and economies leads to a much more fragmented market compared to what is typical in the West. While we find regulatory differences between states in the US, the insurance industry operates predominantly in English and is entrenched in a culture that doesn't vary too dramatically from coast to coast. The differences across cultures in Asia, however, have a huge impact on how insurance operates. In Muslim-dominated regions like Indonesia or Malaysia, for example, insurance is expected to comply with Islamic law through Takaful, an insurance concept based on mutual cooperation. Other Asian markets, however, do not follow this mandated structure.

Economically, Asia ranges from highly developed to emerging markets, resulting in varied insurance penetration rates. Each Asian country has its unique regulatory body and rules for insurance.

Companies must navigate these complexities, often requiring a high degree of localization in their solutions and strategies. This has resulted in a wider variety of InsurTech models and solutions compared to the more homogeneous Western markets.

InsurTech is set to play a pivotal role in navigating the challenges and seizing the opportunities of Asia's insurance landscape. InsurTech often facilitates a more personalized, customer-centric approach, allowing insurers to tailor their products and services according to individual needs, thereby enhancing customer experience and retention.

The Insurance industry must adapt to each local landscape and define its own future. This is something we have seen happening in many other industries. Social media and e-commerce, for example, emerged in the US as technological advancements as widespread internet accessibility began to shape a new digital era. Amazon and eBay pioneered e-commerce, revolutionizing how businesses and consumers interact and transact. Simultaneously, social media platforms such as MySpace and Facebook transformed communication, creating a virtual space where users could interact, share content, and create online communities.

In contrast, China's journey in the realm of social media and e-commerce developed slightly differently. Alibaba, established in 1999, led the e-commerce boom, while Tencent's QQ and later WeChat redefined social media. WeChat, in particular, established an innovative model by integrating social media, e-commerce, and digital payment systems, leading to a holistic social and commercial ecosystem. The seamless fusion of these elements has since been widely adopted across Asia and the Insurance industry has understood the potential to add yet another element to those super apps.

Tech giants like PhonePe, Lazada, and Grab started offering financial services, including insurance, to their massive user bases. These digital platforms have been identified as a new channel for insurance distribution, reaching a broad audience in a personalized, convenient, and efficient manner.

What also plays a role here is the region's demographics. If we are looking at some of the Asian markets with a large and growing middle class, as well as many young, tech-savvy consumers, the demand for digital, easily accessible, and flexible insurance products is high and led to the rise of alternative forms of distribution.

In many parts of developing Asia, particularly in rural areas, insurance penetration is low, and traditional distribution channels have failed to reach these potential customers. Asia's rapid digital transformation has paved the way for e-commerce platforms, ride-hailing apps, and fintech companies to offer insurance products seamlessly within their platforms.

Moreover, in parts of Asia where insurance penetration is low, embedded insurance concepts can play a crucial role in bridging the coverage gap. By integrating insurance into everyday products and services, providers can introduce insurance to individuals who might not have sought it out otherwise, thus extending coverage to previously underserved markets.

However, I also want to shine some light on the more mature markets in Asia as I believe there are many lessons to be learned as well. Japan, for example, is a highly mature market that has many ties to America. US Fortune 500 insurer Aflac, for example, generates about 70% of its revenue in Japan and, taking any currency challenges out of the equation, can consider this a very stable revenue stream with customers holding their policies for about 20 years, on average.[7]

While Japan, with its aging population, isn't considered one of Asia's growth markets and might not have the same appetite for innovation, it is still one of the world's largest insurance markets with one of the highest insurance penetration rates.[8] It is an interesting case to watch and understand how insurers are reacting to the challenges this country is facing. I believe many Western countries are well advised to start taking note of the Japanese example as they are also facing a rapidly ageing population.

---

[7] Trentmann, Nina, "Aflac's Income is mostly in Yen," *The Wall Street Journal*, 25 May 2023.
[8] "Insurance Industry in Japan," Statista, 25 May 2023.

I have been following InsurTech and Insurance innovation developments in Asia closely for roughly the past decade. With the Asia InsurTech Podcast, we have talked to over 50 insurtechs about how they are shaping the insurance industry in their country or region.

We have also talked to investors and insurance executives working for incumbents about the integration of InsurTech. This often requires significant investment, a willingness to embrace new ways of doing business, and potentially a reshaping of the industry's regulatory frameworks. Therefore, the rise of InsurTech also signals a period of disruption and adjustment. While this introduces a level of uncertainty, it is precisely this type of creative destruction that paves the way for progress and growth.

It is clear that InsurTech is not merely an optional extra for insurers operating in the Asian market. It is increasingly becoming an essential component of their strategy for success.

Some argue that the insurtech wave has reached its peak and is in decline. In 2022, InsurTech funding globally fell by over 50% and funding in Asian insurtechs fell to US$1.3 billion in 2022 from US$2.6 billion the year before. However, 2022 also saw a new record high of M&A exits for Asian insurtechs, so the story may not be as bleak as the decrease in funding suggests.[9]

I believe InsurTech is *not* dead, we have simply reached a new maturity level. We have gone from disruption to evolution. Established insurance players have understood the power of InsurTech and are following a strategy of acquiring insurtechs instead of building needed solutions inhouse themselves. In many cases, we have reached the implementation stage of the innovation that is InsurTech. This cyclical progression is an inherent part of our evolving civilization, where we continuously learn and adapt in order to innovate.

In the next section, we delve into the world of case studies, examining the paths taken by various players in the Asian insurance industry, the challenges they've overcome, and the triumphs they've celebrated. Each story is a testament to Asia's dynamic insurance landscape and a powerful demonstration of the potential of InsurTech.

---

[9] "State of Insurtech: Global 2022 Recap," CBInsights, 26 May 2023.

II. Bringing Asia's Success Stories to a Global Audience

Regardless of whether you are in Asia or elsewhere in the world, our lives are constantly changing, insurance is changing, and we all can learn a lot from analyzing the most innovative organizations and their core principals.

This section of the book presents the stories of various companies that started in the insurance industry in Asia and are at the forefront in designing the future of insurance in their market and globally.

While sharing these case studies, it's crucial to understand that these organizations aren't outliers. They are not immune to the challenges the whole industry is facing. Although they might not face the same challenges and complexities as you, they probably deal with other obstacles that you're spared from. At the end of the day, we all function within the same industry, subjected to similar dynamics. Therefore, their examples can inspire and guide you in strategizing your business advancement.

The case studies are organized in such a way that they narrate the company's journey, share the developments and outcomes, and highlight key takeaways. Each case concludes with a summary titled "Foundations for The Future," spotlighting pivotal factors that led to the study's positive result.

Each company has gained unique insights from their journey, and this is where the true value of these case studies lies. The intent is not to prescribe specific solutions, instead, the goal is to present examples of successful evolution in contexts that may mirror your current circumstances. These key learnings can aid us in overcoming the challenges we face and facilitate our progression.

I urge you to make notes, contemplate the specific circumstances at your organization, consider the applicability of these case studies, and reflect on how the insights and takeaways could influence your objectives. Engage in discussions about what you've read with a colleague, supervisor, or peer, and challenge yourself to visualize how you can drive evolution in your environment despite the obstacles and potential disruptive threats.

4. YAS

Most people are familiar with the Greek mythology of the Trojan Horse, one of history's most famous deceptions to capture the uncapturable. The myth is set during the Trojan War, between Greece and Troy. Despite their best military efforts, the Greeks were not able to conquer the city of Troy, so they came up with an ingenious deception plan to infiltrate the city. They built a large wooden horse and gifted it to the Trojans as a peace offering. When the Trojans took the horse inside the city gates, little did they know that hidden inside were armed Greek soldiers. At night, the soldiers emerged and captured the city of Troy.

While the original Trojan Horse myth had a devastating outcome for Troy, I believe we can use the analogy for hidden benefits that are only revealed after the passage of time. Hong Kong-based insurtech startup YAS reminds me of such an example.

YAS launched in 2020 and entered the Hong Kong market in May of 2021. Early on, the startup secured a strategic partnership to capture a new market segment as part of what I would call a 'Trojan Horse' strategy.

YAS was founded by Andy Ann, Kelvin Cheung and William Lee with the goal of reinventing insurance by being truly 'user centric' – a term, I feel, we have been talking a lot about in the insurance industry over the past decade. Despite the talk, in Ann's experience, insurers are still heavily product focused which is often due to corporate culture, legacy systems, and strict regulation.

Before starting YAS, Ann and Lee had their own analytics and consulting companies and were working with corporate clients, including insurers. What inspired them to start their own business-to-consumer (B2C) business was the rise of virtual banks and the gap they saw in the insurance market in terms of digitization and mobile-first approaches.

Ann explained that today, usability is the most important factor, with consumers becoming increasingly accustomed to one-touch, seamless user experiences – such as those provided by companies like Spotify, Uber and Netflix. These services have significantly changed customer expectations globally, and Ann believes that insurance also has the potential to be downloadable and streamable – as in on-demand insurance that can be turned on and off and is sharable between friends and family.

> "We believe in the future, our generation will experience with one-touch – you are insured. We believe that insurance should be downloadable ...it should be streamable...and we also think that insurance can be sharable."
>
> – Andy Ann
> Co-Founder, YAS

However, the Hong Kong insurance market is still widely dominated by traditional distribution models. Despite there being over 116,000 licensed insurance intermediaries in the Hong Kong market as of April 30th 2023,[10] digital penetration is estimated to be below 2%, according to Ann. Such a lack of digital penetration suggested significant opportunity for innovation to YAS's founders. The question for them was how to take advantage of this opportunity.

Looking at successful technology companies in the B2C space, Ann identified three factors that he believes are essential to building a successful business with the potential to achieve unicorn status, meaning a company valuation of over one billion US dollars:

1. Great product that addresses customer needs.
2. Loyalty programs to engage with customers.
3. A community were people come together.

Ann believes that these three aspects are what made companies like Tencent and Alibaba successful and turned them into hyper growth tech giants. Compared to organizations in the financial services industry, tech companies have excelled at understanding customer needs, being empathetic and designing seamless customer touchpoints.

Following these guidelines, the first step in building YAS was to understand what it is that customers really want and need.

---

[10] "Statistics – Insurance Intermediary License," Hong Kong Insurance Authority, 30 May 2023.

One of Ann's existing businesses is an analytics company that aggregates data from social media, blogs and forums, allowing it to identify trends and pain points. One of the major trends it identified was that more people are engaging in outdoor activities.

This trend had further been fueled by the outbreak of the COVID-19 pandemic and the resulting public health restrictions on the freedom of movement and international travel, leading more people to seek outdoor activities at a local or national level. Ann explained that during COVID-19 in Hong Kong, sales of bicycles went up 400%, while hiking and outdoor activities doubled.

This naturally led to an increase in accidents for those participating in these activities and people started exchanging advice online about how to stay safe. Using those insights, YAS identified one of their target markets being people engaging in outdoor activities.

Inspired by the mobile-first strategy of virtual banks, YAS set up its operations to be fully digital, selling exclusively through their mobile app. Despite only holding an insurance agency license, YAS decided to design their own products to ensure they are addressing the customer needs identified by their data. These products include low-cost personal accident protection for riding a motorcycle or bicycle, going for a hike or a run, as well as coverage while commuting.

Products are designed as a per-trip cover. For example, customers can buy 10 cycling trips that will cover them for the specified number of bicycle rides of up to six hours per trip. Rates start at HK$38 (<US$5) per trip for bicycle rides and HK$15 (<US$2) for hiking trips.

Premiums this low do not leave a lot of room for margin and are difficult to scale up to support a business. Offering micro insurance products is only commercially viable if business processes are fully automated and distribution costs are kept to a minimum. Therefore, a critical key to success is identifying the right distribution strategy. In addition, YAS needed something to distribute in the first place, meaning they had to identify an underwriting partner since they only held an insurance agency license. Building carrier and distributor relationships would be critical steps for YAS to take as it built its mobile-first business model.

The second factor in Ann's guidelines to building a successful company are loyalty programs. However, YAS did not only look at building their own loyalty program, but to partner with already-established loyalty programs to leverage their existing scale and member affinity. YAS would then offer members insurance products as part of the loyalty program. What they ended up building is the idea of 'loyalty as insurance', which is the basis for their Trojan Horse strategy.

Given YAS' target market of active people in the outdoors, the startup was looking for a partner that serves this market. Hong Kong has many hiking trails and, according to Ann, a quarter million hikers take the bus to hiking sites every weekend over other forms of transportation. Hong Kong has a very advanced public transport system and customers often have the choice between taking the mass transit rail (MTR) or different bus services. To differentiate from other services, the Kowloon Motor Bus (KMB), which carries over two million passengers each day,[11] has rolled out a loyalty program for their customers who hold monthly passes.

YAS' proposition was to offer these monthly pass holders a "free" coverage, as part of KMB's loyalty program. Coverage includes up to HK$5,000 (~US$640) of cover for medical fees for injuries while being on a KMB bus and up to HK$2,000 (~US$255) for lost or stolen items. Premiums would be covered by the rider's accrued loyalty points, meaning there was no explicit cost to the customer, hence the term 'loyalty as insurance'.

At first, KMB was not convinced of the insurance loyalty program as they were worried that people might associate danger with using their services if they offer free insurance protection.

However, YAS did not give up that easily and went back to pitch their hiking insurance product, pointing out that KMB transports over a quarter million hikers every weekend. Offering insurance protection is what could differentiate KMB from their competitors and by concentrating on the risks of hiking rather than inadvertently implying some increased risk associated with the bus company they addressed the concern about sending the wrong message about riding the bus. On the contrary, by offering hiking protection, KMB builds the image of a caring company that understands its customers' interests and the risks they face even after their journey with KMB. This argument resolved KMB's concern and is what got YAS over the line to start negotiations.

---

[11] "Kowloon Motor Bus," Transportation Department, The Government of the Hong Kong Special Administrative Region, as of 30 May, 2023.

To come to an agreement, KMB had to first confirm with their existing insurance provider that they had no interest in offering this type of protection. Not many insurers are keen to venture into the micro insurance space, so, unsurprisingly, KMB's existing partner showed no interest.

The next challenge was the legal aspect of the partnership and the responsibilities of the parties involved. For example, in case of complaints, who will be contacted and who is liable? Naturally, KMB did not want to overload their customer service team with insurance-related requests from customers. Clarifying these aspects is what took YAS the longest to resolve and demonstrates how complex the insurance industry is compared to other industries. Working through such legal requirements are often what puts small startups under survival pressure given how long those issues can take to resolve and the potential liabilities they can create. Having the resources and knowledge to understand the legal implications for their products, including the liabilities and responsibilities they might be assuming, was a strategic imperative for YAS. In the case of the partnership with KMB, YAS is responsible for customer service, including claims management, and is the liable party should something go wrong with the product.

In addition to the negations with KMB, YAS was facing another challenge. As mentioned already, the startup only holds an insurance agency license and needed an underwriter for their proposed products. To secure the partnership, KMB required YAS to present an underwriter so there was an actual product to partner on. YAS had been searching for an underwriting partner for a while, but not many insurance incumbents are willing or technically able to partner with an insurtech for an idea as novel as this. YAS only identified three insurers in Hong Kong that can work with advanced application programming interfaces (APIs), which was a crucial component of YAS' plan to integrate with the bus company, so the universe of potential partners was extremely small.

Just in time for the partnership deal with KMB, YAS was in negotiations with Italian insurer Generali, who not only had the technical abilities required but was also willing to underwrite a micro insurance product. Ann shared that Generali was the right insurance partner because of their forward thinking and a culture and mindset that embraces innovation.

Working with a startup on new concepts comes with risks and requires a high level of agility. The team at Generali was willing to work together to push for innovation and allowed YAS to test their concept while being aware and accepting of the potential risk of failure. Ann explained that "failing forward is the only way to push through innovation and break through conventional business models."

> "Failing forward is the only way to push through innovation and break through conventional business models."
>
> – Andy Ann
> Co-Founder, YAS

Given the challenges of selling insurance solely via digital channels, and considering the products don't yield a significant margin or generate substantial premiums, Generali would only consent to underwrite the program if YAS secured a partnership with KMB, which guaranteed high traffic.

"It was basically the perfect storm," Ann noted of the catch 22 YAS was in. Despite both parties making their participation contingent on that of the other, YAS managed to get both partnerships signed within three months. This took frequent, open communication from YAS to both of their partners, and careful management of the timing of everything.

It is reminiscent of the story in *Volume II* of this series, when Kin insurance needed to secure licenses for its admitted insurance carrier, but also needed funding in place to capitalize the carrier. The licenses couldn't be granted without the capital, and the capital could not be issued without the licenses. This chicken and egg dilemma seemed to stretch on for ages to Kin, but they managed through it with vigilance and astute project and relationship management, just as YAS did here.

While it may have seemed to be a long time for a startup, this was a significant departure from the timelines we tend to see in the insurance industry, especially when it involves an incumbent insurer, a brand new insurtech startup, and a partner from another industry. This is even more impressive when you consider the technical aspects of this partnership, and that one of the players is a government entity.

For this three-sided partnership to work, YAS had to integrate with KMB and Hong Kong's public transport payment system, Octopus, as well as with Generali. While the integration challenges with Generali could be solved through offline solutions to a certain degree (e.g., through monthly bordereaux reporting, which is essentially spreadsheets of transactions and policies), the integration with Octopus had to be fully digital. With two million passengers per day, YAS had to be able to efficiently identify eligibility for their 'loyalty as insurance' cover and onboard members seamlessly.

To do this, they had to integrate the Octopus payment logic via API into their application process and collect the applicant's Hong Kong ID card details. This was essential to verify the applicant's eligibility for the 'free' cover, provide reliable conversion data to KMB, confirm who is paying for the coverage, and collect the required information for Generali's Know Your Customer (KYC) process.

Because YAS is offering instant coverage once a passenger has opted in, the team had to automate the entire process starting within KMB's mobile app, all the way to Generali to issue the policy, and back to the user to confirm coverage quickly and seamlessly.

After confirming eligibility for the free policy, the relevant data for the KYC process is transmitted automatically to Generali as the underwriter. Policy issuance is automated and timestamped using blockchain technology which facilitates having one source of truth about identity, location and the start of coverage. The policy confirmation is then sent to the customer instantly in KMB's app. This covers the underwriting process, but YAS had to implement a process for claims management, as well.

With the pieces in place as of July 2021, passengers using KMB's monthly pass could sign up for YAS' loyalty as insurance cover. Signs on the outside of KMB busses and on the back of the bus seats inform people about the coverage. By scanning a QR code people can find out more information on the coverage and get the link to sign up. They might not have been aware that such a cover existed or that they needed it, but when presented with free insurance cover hidden inside their bus ticket, people learned about the benefits, and opted in.

With a single partnership, YAS has secured potential access and exposure to KMB's two million daily riders. Monthly pass holders who decide to sign up for the free coverage are not only introduced to the hidden insurance benefits but also to YAS as a brand.

In addition, YAS has the potential to convert monthly pass holders into being its own users more broadly. In order to receive the insurance coverage, users must sign up for the YAS platform and therefore instantly become members of YAS' mobile app. Once on the app, users can buy additional coverage based on their needs.

What is very powerful in this example is that people get an essentially free cover that triggers them to think about the benefits of insurance and puts them in the right mindset to consider buying additional products. It also puts them into the platform to be able to act on that consideration.

This is where the Trojan Horse nature of their strategy comes in. YAS was able to hide an entry level product within a product unrelated to insurance in order to capture a new market. According to Ann, YAS has a conversion rate of 35% of monthly pass holders and is signing up around 600 new users per week.

However, this is not a Greek myth where YAS can hold the captured market hostage, and YAS' journey is only just beginning. This is where Ann's third success factor comes in – building a community.

YAS developed a strategy of building communities around each product. For example, for their hiking coverage, the startup is engaging with hiking clubs and is producing content for social media. Brand endorsers wearing YAS t-shirts produce videos for social media where they share their hiking experiences, giving recommendations for new routes and tips on how to stay safe.

In addition, YAS partners with related ecosystems. They have signed agreements with 50 bike shops to offer mutual discounts to their members. Bike shop members get a discount on coverage from YAS, and YAS members get a discount with the bike shop. According to Ann, YAS' retention rate is roughly 79%, and he cites their affinity relationships built on strong communities as a key driver of this performance.

While the KMB, hiking and bike shop examples show early signs of market success for YAS, that does not mean the business will be profitable in the long run. It is too early to tell as YAS only commenced operations in 2021. The biggest threat to their profitability will be customer acquisition cost (CAC) – a common challenge for many insurtech startups. Ann explained that YAS' average acquisition cost is US$15, coming down to US$9, and they have a target to get below US$5. Even achieving this target would still leave CAC equal to the average premium for their products (at best), and multiples of YAS' commission on each sale, so their model will depend on retention – another reason why Ann recognizes the importance in his three success factors.

It is important not to write off YAS or similar solutions due to the high relative CAC. After all, insurance is a flow business dependent on retention in general, so it will be important to see how well YAS retains customers and is able to up-sell and cross-sell additional products, and they are building their business with the mechanisms to do both. Ann explains they are aiming for an average revenue per user (ARPU) of US$150.

Hong Kong, with a population of 7.4 million,[12] is a difficult market in which to scale a product, so YAS is branching out to other countries and has set-up offices in Malaysia and Vietnam. Relying again on data analysis, YAS has identified that both countries show a significant population interested in hiking and cycling, and they are planning to enter those markets with offerings similar to those in Hong Kong.

In addition, YAS has raised US$4.5 million in a pre-Series A funding round to expand into other areas including web3. The company has identified the web3 industry as one of the fastest growing sectors globally. With their first product in this space, YAS is offering protection from cyber theft for NFTs (non-fungible tokens) and has again found a strong partner, NFT platform Appreciator.io.

There is a huge potential in partnering with different ecosystems and building a distribution mechanism that brings down acquisition costs over time. Although leveraging the products and customer base of others has its advantages, as shown by the YAS case, it also poses risks since YAS doesn't own those ecosystems or holds underwriting capabilities.

The initial agreement with KMB was only for one year and YAS faced the risk of getting replaced by another provider. However, what is not as easily replaceable is the community and the brand that the company is building, or the digital integration (with Octopus) and customer experience YAS has built to facilitate the program. This increases the switching costs for KMB, helping YAS in their goal of keeping the program going and after the first year it was successfully extended.

So, after the Trojan Horse has entered the gates, it is up to the team hiding inside to keep both users and partners engaged for the long-term.

---

[12] "Population, total - Hong Kong SAR, China," The World Bank, as of 30 May 2023.

Foundations for The Future

- ⚲ Use insights from data analytics to understand gaps in the market and spot trends and growth opportunities in real time.

- ⚲ Never underestimate the legal component. Insurance is a complex, highly regulated industry that is especially difficult to crack for people who haven't worked in this space before.

- ⚲ Loyalty as insurance can be utilized to gain access to a larger customer base by taking cost out of the purchase decision; allowing you to build brand and product awareness with less friction and resistance.

- ⚲ Do not rely on a single partnership for your business model, and ensure you are building value for that partner and their customers to protect the relationships you do have.

5. OneDegree

Looking across the industry, we find a large variety of different insurtechs with no universal technique of categorizing them. I like to form three broad categories: fully licensed insurance carriers, insurance intermediaries focusing on distribution, and enablers – companies providing tech solutions for one or more parts of the insurance value chain enabling insurers to innovate.

With the Asia InsurTech Podcast, Michael Waitze and I have been closely watching the development of the space in Asia since April 2019. We noticed most insurtechs that are able to attract early-stage funding in the Asian market focus on distribution and hold a broker or insurance agent license. The second largest category in our experience are enablers. The rarest category is licensed, full-stack insurers. There are a few well-known examples of this third group like ZhongAn in China, or Acko and Digit in India, but these are exceptions compared to the broader insurtech landscape.

There are good reasons why we do not see as many full-stack carriers. One is the high capital requirements to obtain a license and capitalize the licensed entity. Raising large amounts of money combined with the uncertainty of the business model's success seems like an impossible task. As the capital is generally parked to meet regulatory requirements, it is not usually able to generate the returns venture investors need, making it hard for startups to affordably source the statutory capital required of licensed carriers. In addition, many countries do not grant new insurance licenses or do so extremely rarely. This is certainly the case for Hong Kong.

Hong Kong has 89 P&C insurers with a general insurance license.[13] With a population of only 7.4 million, the Hong Kong Insurance Authority (IA) is understandably very reluctant to approve new carrier licenses. For many years it was only possible to enter the market by acquiring an existing licensed insurer. This changed on September 29th, 2017, when the IA launched a pilot scheme called 'Fast Track' that grants virtual insurance licenses to carriers solely using digital distribution channels. The IA has established two separate virtual licenses, a general insurance license for P&C business and a license for life insurers.[14]

As explained in the previous chapter, online penetration is still very low in Hong Kong, which has most likely led to the decision to establish a virtual insurance license to allow the sale of insurance products exclusively through digital channels. In addition, direct sales channels have the potential to increase the number of protection products available in the market. Hong Kong does have high insurance penetration, however, this is mostly attributed to savings products rather than true insurance, so a solution that expands protection was attractive to regulators.

In 2019, Avo Insurance was the first insurer to be granted a virtual general insurance license. The insurtech has the look and feel of a startup but is actually a joint venture of existing players. Majority-owned by insurance incumbent Asia Insurance, which holds a 51% stake, the company shares leadership with its parent. Winnie Wong helms both Avo Insurance and Asia Insurance as their CEO. Meanwhile, investment firm Hillhouse Capital, owns the remaining 49%.[15]

The inception of Avo Insurance stems from a strategy to penetrate a fresh market segment without diluting the established brand value of Asia Insurance. But delving deeper into that journey is a tale for another occasion.

Instead, I would like to focus on the first *startup* to be granted a virtual general insurance license in Hong Kong and which arguably has

---

[13] "Register of Authorized Insurers," Hong Kong Insurance Authority, as of 30 May 2023.

[14] "InsurTech Corner," Hong Kong Insurance Authority, as of 30 May 2023.

[15] Olano, Gabriel, "Hong Kong grants first virtual general insurance license," *Insurance Business Magazine*, 30 May 2023.

fundamentally helped to establish the virtual insurance license in the first place – OneDegree.

Founded by Alvin Kwock and Alex Leung, OneDegree received their virtual general insurance license in April 2020. The journey to achieve this milestone has been beyond challenging and against all odds.

Leung is an actuary by training and has extensive experience in the insurance industry, having worked for consulting firms, insurers and insurtechs in the US and in Asia. Kwock, at the time working as an investment banker, saw opportunity in the insurance space and was passionate about founding an insurtech. To learn more about the insurtech landscape, he did a tour across the US, meeting people from different insurtechs. This is when the co-founders got introduced to each other. The two discussed how the Asian insurance market is lagging behind the US on digital transformation and the opportunities this might present to insurtechs in this part of the world.

There are divergent schools of thought on the levels of innovation in Asia. Some consider it behind digitally, while others believe it is one of the most innovative regions globally. I believe there is a bit of truth to both.

Considering the low labor costs in many Asian countries combined with a growing insurance market, automation of existing processes might not have the same relative importance in Asia as in other markets like the US. Digitization efforts in the US and Western Europe initially started not to innovate the business model but to cut operating expense. While this may lead to higher levels of digitization, it does not necessarily foster innovation. In an environment where your biggest objective is to cut cost, the necessary creativity to think outside the box and in new dimensions is often difficult to achieve.

In Asia, on the other hand, we find many growth markets. Where there is growth, there is room to be creative. In my experience, insurers in the US are often ahead in terms of digitizing operations, while insurers and especially insurtechs in Asia are more creative when it comes to developing new business and distribution models and ways to make insurance accessible to new market segments. In addition, developing markets often come with a greenfield space, allowing for the creation of new business models without legacy constraints or competition.

Looking at Hong Kong, a very mature market, Kwock and Leung believed that there was a massive opportunity in the underpenetrated digital insurance space. However, while they initially focused on technology adoption and distribution, they quickly realized that this is not the real issue the industry is facing. That, they believed, is about launching meaningful products based on customer needs and the ability to bring those products to the market fast.

By only focusing on distribution, Kwock and Leung would not solve any issues around product design. Their ambition, however, was to fundamentally change the insurance industry and control the product innovation process from initial development to subsequent iterations. This is when they arrived at the conclusion that they had to start their own insurance company if they wanted to control product design and have the autonomy to experiment across the entire insurance value chain. An ambitious if not impossible endeavor, considering that, at that time, there were no successful examples of fully licensed insurtech startups in Asia other than ZhongAn, which had just started in China.

"We really wanted to own the product and have control of all decisions on the product itself. And it has proven to really be a key value for us as an organization. Why we can be so fast in iterating and changing our product and ensuring product-market fit is because we control what we do on underwriting criteria, on the pricing, on the design or product. Therefore, decision making is a lot faster," Leung shared.

Inspired by new digital insurance concepts in the US, Kwock and Leung wanted to focus on products that can be distributed digitally. However, the million-dollar question was, what type of products can be successfully sold online. Leung shared the three factors that he believed influence whether a product can be effectively sold online:

1. The simplicity and transparency of a product: The product, its benefits and the terms and conditions must be easily understandable for consumers.

2. The target market and its financial literacy: The target market must be mature enough with sufficient purchasing power and a high degree of financial literacy. Hong Kong, at least when compared to developing countries in Asia, is a very mature market with high financial literacy.

3. The type of product: People need a key motivation to buy and shop on their own online. According to Leung, this applies to mandatory insurance products, like motor insurance, or coverage for things people love and want to protect.

This led OneDegree to start with pet insurance. Pet insurance fulfills all of Leung's requirements: it can be structured as a very simple and straightforward product; people in Hong Kong love their pets dearly; those who own pets in Hong Kong are often educated and in higher income brackets.

Unlike in some other locations, pet ownership in Hong Kong can signal a higher level of affluence. This stems from it being one of the most densely populated cities in the world, with average living space of public rental housing of just 146 sq ft (13.6 sqm).[16] Owning a pet takes up scarce additional space and requires approval from landlords. Therefore, it is often a luxury reserved for the wealthier population in Hong Kong. Leung explained that pet parents are very likely more affluent, have a high degree of financial literacy and disposable income for things they love and want to protect.

Pet insurance is not new to Hong Kong and has been available in the market for over a decade. The product has been traditionally sold by agents and was not regarded as a lucrative sector.

Leung's experience from the US market, however, suggested that there is massive opportunity in pet insurance. Pet insurance has shown steady market growth in the US reaching US$3.2 billion in 2023 with 16.5% annualized market size growth from 2018 to 2023.[17] Comparing those experiences to the Hong Kong market, Kwock and Leung believed that pet insurance was not being marketed the right way in their home market.

With a target product decided, it took the company the next four years to actually launch their pet insurance product, having to overcome several major challenges along the way, including acquiring a general insurance license and raising the capital required. These were intertwined problems because you cannot have one without the other.

Starting an insurance company as a startup is certainly a balancing act with two clashing extremes. On the one hand, you have the startup

---

[16] "Average living space of public rental housing tenants in Hong Kong from 2007 to 2021," Statista, 30 May 2023.
[17] "Pet Insurance in the US," IBIS World, 30 May 2023.

approach of bootstrapping and being as cost efficient as possible. On the other hand, you have the necessity to convince people of your credibility and that you have the experience and knowledge needed. To build a full-stack insurer, a wide range of skillsets are required, and the team had to convince investors and the regulator that they are able to attract and retain experienced insurance professionals that know the industry well to join the team and the board.

When trying to convince the regulator of a highly risk averse industry to support your idea, perception matters. In the end, insurance is about risk management and people working in the industry are, for a good reason, often highly risk averse. Startups, conversely, are about risk in their very nature, and have a 90% chance of failing.[18]

What certainly did not make it any easier for OneDegree was the fact that their first office was in an industrial building in Hong Kong. "The building was scary. The hallway didn't really have lights and we only had a tiny conference room," Leung remembered.

Under such circumstances, OneDegree was trying to convince the regulator and give them confidence that the team had what it takes to build a full-stack insurer. The regulator was used to multinational conglomerates with deep resources and controls, not to a tiny startup operating from a poorly lit, run-down-looking building. "That was extremely difficult," Leung recalled.

With the strong belief in their business model and confidence in the combined knowledge of the team, OneDegree pushed forward and submitted their original business plan to the IA for a general insurance license in December 2016. Being the first technology startup that has taken on the challenge of acquiring a license, there were lessons to be learned on both sides.

The team at OneDegree worked closely with the regulator to analyze developments in the US and other markets and discussed the implications for Hong Kong to understand how the local insurance market might develop in the future. Both parties benefitted from each other's expertise. While the regulator helped the startup understand the requirements for obtaining an insurance license, the OneDegree team provided consultation on trends and developments in other markets.

---

[18] "90% Of Startups Fail: Here's What You Need To Know About The 10%," Forbes, 30 May 2023.

Toward the end of 2017, the IA came up with a first framework for a virtual insurance license.

This is a reminder that it is not only insurers being impacted by a rapidly changing environment. I have spoken to regulators across Asia about new challenges coming from changes in consumer behavior, new technologies like blockchain, and the need and urgency to review data privacy laws in a digital environment. What I found was that often insurtechs are the ones challenging the *status quo*, inspiring the industry to think in new directions.

In Hong Kong, the IA made the decision that the requirements to apply for its new virtual insurance license would be the same as applying for a traditional license. From the IA's perspective, this decision was made in order to ensure sustainability of operations and protect consumer interests. Leung sums it up when he says, "From the key person perspective, from the capital perspective, from the system readiness, really everything on the insurance setup is the same except with the additional requirement that, because we are functioning in a digital world, cyber security plays a much bigger part. The only other difference is the restriction that we cannot work with traditional intermediaries."

Like any new frameworks, the virtual insurance license continues to evolve. For example, some virtual insurers have received permission to sell their products through other digital channels and treat them as digital agents. Initially all players started off on the same ground and were only allowed to sell through their own direct channels. I believe we will see more iterations of the new virtual insurance license as the insurance market in Hong Kong keeps evolving and as more players challenge the *status quo*. Regardless of what it looks like at any point in time, the genesis of the virtual license can be traced back to a challenge tackled collaboratively by OneDegree and the regulator.

Simultaneously with their efforts working with the regulator on the possibility to obtain an insurance license, OneDegree had to secure funding to fulfill the capital requirements. As many founders learn, raising money is a full-time job. It took the team at OneDegree two years and over 100 meetings with potential investors before they could confirm their Series A funding round of US$25.5 million in September 2018. This was the largest ever fundraising round for a pre-revenue insurance tech startup in Hong Kong to this point. The startup then extended the round to US$30 million in May 2019.

Leung shared that the key to winning over investors, who had initially said no, was proving his and Kwok's persistency and commitment to this venture, giving investors confidence in the founders' ability to deliver on their plan.

> "We all have very deep skin in the game. It's not just taking other people's money and running with it, but we actually invested a lot of money ourselves. In that early stage, just within our team, we invested close to US$2 million."
>
> – Alex Leung
> Co-Founder,
> OneDegree

Kwok and Leung were able to convince many of the early founding team members to become investors themselves. "We all have very deep skin in the game. It's not just taking other people's money and running with it, but we actually invested a lot of money ourselves. In that early stage, just within our team, we invested close to US$2 million," Leung recalled.

When preparing for the license, OneDegree had to submit a business plan not only to its investors but to the IA as well. The startup had to justify how they planned to reach their projected sales targets, another reminder that starting a licensed insurance company is much more complex than starting an insurance brokerage. The insurance regulator must be convinced that the business model is sustainable and that the company is not going to become insolvent in the foreseeable future or will require constant capital infusions to stay afloat.

A crucial part of OneDegree's business plan of selling pet insurance online was to secure partnerships with go-to veterinarian clinics and hospitals, and partner with strong pet shop brands and pet e-commerce sites as well as NGOs.

Due to the limitations of the virtual insurance license, those partners could not act as agents and actively sell insurance. Instead, they are considered marketing channels only. OneDegree's marketing engagement with those partners ranged from traditional advertisements like placing banner ads on e-commerce sites or posters in clinics and hospitals, to co-marketing and paying referral fees for lead generation.

Leung shared, "For building an insurance business, getting things off the ground can't be just about the technology propositions. Selling insurance is more about your reputation and credibility. So, when we are a new entrant to the market, how do we establish our brand quickly, especially around the pet parents? You must earn their trust – building that trust requires both driving our own brand marketing and leveraging the strong brands that already exist in the market."

With select veterinarian clinics and hospitals, OneDegree has formed deeper relationships, adding them to its network of preferred partners. Those in this network receive preferential treatment for claims processing, which benefits their mutual customers. It is basically the same model that is widely established in human medical care with partnerships between health insurers and healthcare providers they've deemed 'in-network' or auto body repair shops motor insurers include in their network (sometimes referred to as direct repair programs).

OneDegree also partners with NGOs like the SPCA and Hong Kong Dog Rescue to run a number of campaigns including one where you receive free pet insurance when you adopt a pet.

Before being granted their license, OneDegree had to invest in building these marketing channels to secure the partnerships and demonstrate to the IA that their business plan was viable. In other words, the investment the startup had to raise was not only to fulfill the high capital requirements for the license to be granted but also to prepare for the launch and the marketing activities needed. It also meant, OneDegree had to spend on these marketing channels before they even knew if they'd have the ability to actually market a product through them.

The next challenge was finding reinsurers that could support OneDegree in developing their pet insurance products. The team was hoping that reinsurers could provide knowhow on product design and pricing. However, that was not the case, at least not for the Hong Kong market. Instead, the team had to design their products and pricing without reinsurer insight and support. On top of that, they now had to convince the reinsurers to provide backing for these products created by an unproven startup.

Leung shared, "Hong Kong has been selling pet insurance for a long time. But no company has done it well, with no one really seeing sales success. Reinsurers were kind of stuck in the *status quo* mindset of 'that hasn't really worked out in the past, so why do you think you can do it better?' Added to that was this question of the potential success of online sales when that channel had not previously found much traction in Hong Kong versus selling in person."

OneDegree's pet insurance business was launched right after the startup received its license in April 2020. Since then, the company has experienced multi-fold increases in market share of pet insurance in Hong Kong while also helping to quadruple the market size – something that their competitors were not able to achieve even with a decade head start.

OneDegree has indeed revolutionized the underpenetrated pet insurance market in Hong Kong and has built strong partnerships in that space. However, in a market with a population of just 7.4 million people and with only 500,000 pet cats and dogs, an insurer cannot solely focus on this one product line. Bringing in additional products was always crucial to their long-term viability from the beginning, so OneDegree set a strategy to become a multi-line insurer from the start.

Competing in other lines comes with new challenges. The team at OneDegree has continued to research new offerings to cross-sell to its customer base as well as to identify gaps in the market to develop new product propositions. Since the pet insurance launch in 2020, they have subsequently rolled-out fire and home insurance products and developed a critical illness product that can be claimed multiple times as opposed to most of the existing products on the market that only allow customers to claim once.

Marketing a critical illness product is very different to marketing a product like pet insurance. Working in a more developed segment with fiercer competition meant the startup had to identify how to clearly differentiate from other providers and build a strong brand that consumers trust.

The startup had to change its marketing strategy from the niche pet insurance approach. Instead of partnering with selected partners and leveraging the community aspect, OneDegree had chosen a mass-marketing strategy for their critical illness cover.

Leung explained that, especially when launching a new product, there are significant costs for marketing and branding involved. This was the case for the upfront expenses for the customer acquisition campaigns and promotions with their pet insurance partnerships and the mass-marketing advertisement of the critical illness coverage. The insurer started investing in traditional marketing tools like television, radio, and billboards to build brand awareness. This comes at high costs that the startup would have to see payback over time.

According to Leung, costs for customer acquisitions are going down for them as they've matured, and the benefits of their initial investment will show. He believes once the brand has reached a certain critical mass, word of mouth and referrals will kick in while their renewal base sustains them. That also meant that after building customer awareness and a brand, OneDegree had to focus on their customer experience to ensure they can retain customers they attracted and benefit from referrals to new customers.

OneDegree runs a variety of member-get-member campaigns where the insurer offers discounts, cash vouchers or gifts if you refer another customer. These referral schemes have consistently delivered a new policy conversion rate of over 25%. This is not only an effective customer acquisition program but also allows the insurer to track customer associations via referrals.

In addition, the company is applying social listening to understand what people are saying about their brand and if they recommend the brand to friends and family. For example, the insurer actively tracks and monitors all mentions of its brand and discussion of its products across news, online forums, and social media. All this information helps guide OneDegree on where to invest their limited resources.

> "No matter how much research we have done ... really nothing beats what we learn once we get to the market. We have to stay in listening and learning mode, even after launch."
>
> – Alex Leung
> Co-Founder,
> OneDegree

What struck me as a major difference to most insurance incumbents is the way OneDegree looks at customer experience. The startup is not only interested to learn how people think about the service the company provides but also how satisfied their customers are with the overall product design. Listening to what people say on social media in addition to the insights the team gets through their customer service channels and customer conversion funnel help them improve their product offering. "No matter how much research we have done, for an insurance product or launch events, really nothing beats what we learn once we get to the market. We have to stay in listening and learning mode, even after launch." Leung advised.

Being able to react quickly to feedback from customers is what Leung described as their key competitive advantage. Afterall, this was the reason why the startup decided to pursue the difficult journey of starting a licensed insurer in a market that did not allow for it anymore in the first place. They wanted to control the underwriting, pricing and product design, so decision making and execution would be much faster.

As a result, they launch a new version of their product based on feedback from the market every two to three months.

This continuous product iteration demonstrates how different the corporate culture of OneDegree is compared to many existing players. Most incumbent insurers launch a new or revised product once a year. Product innovation is often limited by technology capabilities, making it not only costly to launch new products but also difficult to administer different tariffs or rates within a product.

Given the complex and expensive nature of product development and launch processes, insurers are keen on ensuring they're on the right trajectory. Consequently, many have begun integrating methodologies such as focus groups and design thinking, in addition to their internal working groups and committees. However, what Leung was suggesting is that no matter how much research you conduct before going live, the best feedback comes after the product launches. This requires flexibility and responsiveness to launch and adjust as you learn. For most companies that lack the flexibility, this is an opportunity they miss out on due to their long, resource-heavy product launch cycles.

Another approach that is unique to OneDegree is that the marketing and product teams work together. Leung explained that their team wanted to eliminate the ongoing dispute many insurers face where each team blames the other for low sales numbers or other poor results. Within OneDegree, everybody works together on product development and the marketing proposition. This ensures a marketable product is designed from the start, marketing plans accurately capture the true value of the product that is being sold, and market learnings inform decisions and changes quickly, allowing for better responsiveness post-launch.

In addition to the B2C business, OneDegree also has been developing a B2B proposition, with over 10 logistic platform providers in Hong Kong including Buyandship, Pickupp, and Shipgo. OneDegree provides coverage for property damage, ship-and-return, and missing and lost deliveries. E-commerce and delivery have been booming in Hong Kong since COVID-19, making these B2B offerings strong performers for OneDegree. Leung explained that conversion rates for embedded insurance can be very high and, once set up right, can provide a steady stream of business without the need for additional marketing, making them efficient and sustainable business models.

At first glance, the B2B business appears much simpler with fewer obstacles. There is no need to invest in extensive marketing activities as the platforms are responsible for marketing the product. Building a strong brand might also not be as important, saving on that expense. However, betting on only a few partnerships without the control of the ecosystem also comes with its own risks, as discussed in the previous chapter.

Leung explained, to have a sustainable business, insurers must drive their own differentiation and be able to balance the results and lifecycles of different lines of business. Offering different lines of business through various distribution channels as well as owning their own customer base helps OneDegree minimize the net risk to the enterprise by balancing and countering risks inherent in any one area. This would not have been possible for them if they remained a strictly B2C pet insurer.

In addition, these two sources of business complement each other in different ways. For example, having their own customer base helps in negotiating with platform providers as it makes OneDegree a potential source of new business in addition to being an insurance partner. It also helps give credibility to OneDegree as a trustworthy partner since they already have market proof of their ability to deliver.

While the B2B business has been valuable for OneDegree, Leung circled back to one more reason why their B2C business is crucial to the overall success of the company. He believes engaging in the B2C sector is imperative for fostering innovation. The team at OneDegree is continuously trying to figure out how they can crack a market and how to convert customers of competitors to become their customers. They constantly speak to their customers to understand how they can improve their products and services. It is a great challenge that forces the team to learn and grow through being directly engaged in competing for each customer they win, and to keep each customer they already have.

In other words, the B2C business is what keeps the team on their toes, which is crucial in the fast-moving insurtech space and for a small player trying to take market share from multi-billion-dollar competitors while growing the market as a whole through new approaches to it.

OneDegree has achieved annual sales growth of 150-1700% in Hong Kong from inception to April 2023, with over 200,000 paid users from its B2C and B2B business. In addition, the startup has ventured into new business areas. The team has launched OneInfinity, a digital asset insurance product for crypto exchanges and custodians; is venturing into the technology business with IXT, an enterprise platform that offers a suite of solutions based on an open API architecture to launch new products, enhance operational agility, and facilitate ecosystem partnerships; and Cymetrics, a cyber security software-as-a-service solution. In June 2023, the group announced it has raised an additional US$27 million, bringing the total amount raised to US$97 million.

Foundations for The Future

◉ Starting a fully licensed insurer is a long, complex, and costly journey. It requires a team of experienced professionals with various skillsets, large amounts of funding and even larger amounts of resilience and commitment.

◉ When trying to raise large amounts of funding from investors, it helps to demonstrate how committed you are to the venture by putting your own capital at risk.

◉ No matter the amount of research you conduct beforehand, feedback from customers after a launch will always be more valuable and insightful – though you must ensure you can respond timely and meaningfully.

◉ B2B and B2B2C plays can be solid performers, but even those who lack a B2C play should consider ways to stay close to buyers to keep the flow of insights and ideas into their business so they don't miss opportunities to improve or change.

6. Qoala

Indonesia is often described as one of the most promising markets in Southeast Asia. It is the world's fourth-most populous country with a population of over 270 million people, of which 50% are under the age of 30. Indonesia has been experiencing rapid economic growth in recent years, with its GDP reaching US$1.19 trillion in 2021,[19] making it the largest economy in Southeast Asia. With its young and growing population, Indonesia presents numerous opportunities for businesses and investors.

The insurance industry in Indonesia has experienced steady growth as well, with total premiums reaching Rp 520 trillion (~US$35 billion) in 2021.[20] However, compared to other markets, including many developing countries, insurance penetration, which is a measure of premium as a percent of GDP, is still low. In 2021, Indonesia had an insurance penetration of just 1.6% compared to 12.4% in the USA and 4.2% in India.[21]

This penetration is against a backdrop of strong GDP per capita vs. other developing Asian nations. In 2021, GDP per capita in Indonesia was at US$4,333 while it was only US$2,257 in India.[22] Considering that Indonesia has double the income of India yet only half the insurance penetration, this suggests massive growth opportunities in the country.

Indeed, Indonesia presents a lot of potential in the insurance space, and it is in the country's interest to increase insurance penetration as

---

[19] GDP Indonesia, The World Bank, as of 16 March 2023.
[20] "Value of premiums written in the insurance industry of Indonesia," Statista, 25 April 2023.
[21] Insurance indicators: Penetration, OECD Stats, as of 25 April 2023.
[22] GDP per capita, The World Bank, as of 25 April 2023.

Harshet Lunani, co-founder and CEO of Qoala explained. He said, "I don't think there's any country which has become a great economy without being well insured. Because there's going to be bumps in the road and if your economy and your people are well protected, they will be able to get through the difficult patches and achieve something greater because insurance enables them to take risks."

One of the reasons why insurance penetration is so low in Indonesia is a lack of financial literacy. Many Indonesians have limited knowledge of insurance products and how they can protect themselves, their loved ones, and their assets. As a result, people are less likely to purchase insurance.

In most countries the broader population is forced to engage with insurers when they buy a car or motorbike and therefore learn at least the basics of motor insurance. However, Indonesia is one of very few countries in the world where motor insurance is not mandatory.

Another reason why Indonesia is underpenetrated might has to do with the insurance landscape. Lunani explained that Indonesia's insurance market is "extremely fragmented, probably the most fragmented market in the world. The largest General Insurance player only has around 4% market share and the top five only around 22% while the regulator has issued 140 licenses." In comparison, India has 24 licensed general insurers and the top five hold over 40% market share as of November 2022.[23]

A fragmented market like this leads to two challenges. One is that without prominent brands, the visibility of insurance carriers to consumers is limited and many consumers are therefore unaware of any insurance brands.

The second challenge is traditional insurance distribution. Having so many small players means that many insurers do not have a strong insurance agency force and cannot offer the support agents need in a market like Indonesia that consists of thousands of islands, creating natural barriers between cities, and has such low financial literacy.

I believe Indonesia will define its own future of insurance given that 50% of the population, over 130 million people, is under the age of 30 and have grown up as digital natives. Many of them will buy insurance

---

[23] "Non-life GDPI Flash Figures November 2022," Insurance Regulatory and Development Authority of India, as of 16 May 2023.

for the first time in the coming years and until now traditional players have largely failed to capture this market.

A range of insurtechs have emerged ready to disrupt the market. Harshet Lunani, together with Tommy Martin, founded Qoala in 2018 with the goal to take Indonesia's insurance industry to the next level by educating more people about insurance and increase agent distribution by leveraging technology to create greater opportunities for individuals to sell insurance.

While Qoala always had its main focus on agent distribution the team knew they had to start with educating consumers in order to better support their agent enablement business.

As a private company, educating consumers on a product like insurance isn't an easy task. For one, just thinking about insurance can be very unpleasant. Insurance is often associated with negative events, such as accidents, illness, or death. Thinking about these scenarios can be emotionally taxing for consumers and can make them uncomfortable. This is especially the case in Indonesia where culturally many believe just thinking about such events will invite tragedy to their homes.

In addition, it is often a low priority. Insurable events that are too far in the future are not a top-of-mind concern. Consumers, especially the younger generation, are more focused on other pressing matters, such as work, family, or their hobbies.

In many markets, agents are the ones educating consumers about the importance of managing risks and explaining how people should take action in the form of insurance before it's too late. However, in a market with

> "I think of it like ice cream. When you go to an ice cream store, you see a lot of different flavors, and you want to try a spoonful first. Only if you like it, will you get a scoop. You need that in insurance where you get to try a spoon."
>
> – Harshet Lunani
> Co-Founder, Qoala

a population as unfamiliar with the overall concept of insurance as many Indonesians are, this is a tough sell. Especially for more complex and high-value products that offer a substantial commission to compensate the agents for the many hours of educational work needed to close an insurance policy.

To slowly introduce consumers to the concept of insurance, Qoala has developed a set of bite-sized lifestyle insurance products. Lunani shared, "I think of it like ice cream. When you go to an ice cream store, you see a lot of different flavors, and you want to try a spoonful first. Only if you like it, will you get a scoop. You need that in insurance where you get to try a spoon."

The economics of bite-sized insurance products, however, can be difficult. Agency distribution is mostly not an option as margins are too low to pay a decent commission. Therefore, Qoala is working with partners that serve a large user base. Their partners operate in the travel, ride hailing or e-commerce spaces. However, despite what you might expect, those partners do not need to be online businesses. Qoala works with offline offerings as well. For example, the insurtech offers mobile phone insurance both through large e-commerce platforms and through local brick-and-mortar stores.

What is even more important than the distribution channel is the design of the product. The key is to bundle high demand products of the partner with a bite-sized insurance solution that focuses on a top-of-mind concern of the consumer.

To identify the right product, the team at Qoala analyzes the biggest concerns and worries a consumer has when purchasing the partner's product and how a simple insurance solution can bring peace of mind.

Lunani explained that "if you get into a Grab or Gojek (both ride hailing companies operating in Indonesia), technically you could crash and die. But if you are really worried about that, you will never get into a car in the first place. So, it's not really something that you are concerned about, but you probably have experienced that the driver canceled on you or that you got stuck in traffic. Something that more commonly occurs and is top of mind. We designed a product, that if you get to the airport late, you'll get a free flight."

While death and injury due to an accident are very real scenarios as well and coverage would be advisable especially given the lack of motor insurance in Indonesia, it isn't a primary concern for most consumers. When booking a ride to the airport, most people are more worried that they could miss their flight, and that's where Qoala comes in to offer protection and gently introduce consumers to the concept of insurance.

These types of lifestyle insurance products are new in many markets and Indonesia is no exception. The challenge with products like this is that there is often no historic data available that can be used for pricing. Given the risk averse nature of the insurance industry in general, finding a carrier that is willing to underwrite such a product can be a challenge.

Qoala only holds a broker license in Indonesia and therefore had to find underwriters for the new products they had in mind. To secure insurance partners willing to give this new product offering a try, Qoala had to demonstrate their expertise in product design and willingness to put in significant effort both before and after the product launch.

Going through this initial, what I call, "dating phase," where both partners get to know and start trusting each other, meant that Qoala could not start with an entirely new product that doesn't have any historic data.

If a product like the traffic delay insurance, "is your first product, and you have no track record, you basically have zero chance," explained Lunani. Therefore, the team at Qoala started operations with their insurance partners with classic flight delay insurance, a simpler product with enough historical data available to get successfully through the dating phase.

Once the insurtech had built a relationship with different insurers and demonstrated how real time data can be used to adjust pricing on a monthly or even daily basis, they were in a position to suggest more complex products where no or only limited historical data was available.

For the traffic delay insurance coverage the first stage for the insurtech was to prove that it is possible to develop an algorithm that can be used as a baseline for underwriting and pricing. Lunani explained that the team mapped out different parts of Jakarta, the capital and largest city in Indonesia, monitored traffic and recorded how long it took to get to the airport at different times of day and days of the week. After several months of collecting data, a pattern emerged, and the team developed an algorithm that could be used to identify the risk of getting stuck in traffic and the average time one needs to get to the airport at a certain time and day.

However, this is only the starting point for such a product. Real insights can only be derived from live data once a product has been launched. This data will provide insights how the algorithm needs to be adjusted for the product to become profitable.

Lunani explained that "the good thing with this type of product is, it's not tied to a one-off event like life insurance. With a product like this, you'll have lots of small events, and the payouts are not that big.

You may lose a little bit but because of the frequency of the data, you learn very quickly. You learn rapidly how your algorithm needs to be repriced, and, within a very short timeframe, you could price it up to a point where it is very accurate and sustainable."

Many incumbent insurers are not able to make daily tweaks to a product, mainly due to legacy system constraints. This meant Qoala had to oversee product adjustments for the insurer. At the same time, the team had to be careful not to overstep and keep the team at the insurer in the loop. It was important to get the underwriting partner involved enough for them to feel confident that the young team of the insurtech knew what they were doing but at the same time not to be a burden for the incumbent.

> "... because of the frequency of the data, you learn very quickly. You learn rapidly how your algorithm needs to be repriced, and, within a very short timeframe, you could price it up to a point where it is very accurate and sustainable."
>
> – Harshet Lunani
> Co-Founder, Qoala

It took some time for the teams to find their rhythm and starting the relationship with a simpler product helped the underwriting partner to trust the process and acknowledge the skills the young team brought to the table.

Another lesson learned was to manage expectations. To have the freedom to go through this experimental period of a product with daily adjustments, it is important to find the right partner and to be transparent about how this phase could look like. When entering into an agreement to trial a new product, there needs to be agreement and consent on how long higher loss ratios are acceptable and at what stage the product will be pulled from the market if it is not successful.

Having defined the boundaries and agreeing on an acceptable percentage loss ratio for the first few months gives an insurtech the freedom to experiment while management at the insurance partner can track progress using KPIs they are all aligned on.

Not having such an agreement in place often means the insurtech is under constant pressure from the incumbent and their actuarial team. Afterall, someone at the insurer is responsible for the overall bottom line and therefore can be very sensitive when it comes to high loss ratios.

In addition to building strong relationships with insurance partners, the other component that helped Qoala develop innovative products was support from reinsurers.

Lunani shared that "reinsurers are getting more comfortable with some of these products, because they might have seen it in some other markets given their often-broader geographic lens than primary insurers might have."

Having a reinsurer on their side helped the insurtech convince a local insurer that did not have any experience with such products to work together. It also took away some of the pressure on the local actuarial teams if a reinsurer is on board.

On the other side of the coin is the distribution challenge. As traditional agency distribution isn't an option for such micro-policies, Qoala works with a range of alternative distribution partners.

When embedding an insurance solution into another service or product, you have essentially two design choices, opt-in or opt-out. Opt-out means that the insurance is automatically included and needs to be opted out of by the consumer. Opt-in means the consumer has to make the choice to add the insurance coverage to their purchase.

Lunani emphasized that, while opt-out methods might yield more immediate sales, Qoala prioritizes consumers' conscious decisions, ensuring they recognize the added value of the insurance to the primary product or service. He shared that embedded insurance products that are already priced into the main product are "good for business but are not good for education purposes."

This shows the long-term commitment Qoala has to increase penetration and grow the overall market. While opt-out designs generate higher conversion rates, this is not Qoala's main goal. Their micro-products are a means to an end and only one building block in their mission to increase insurance penetration.

The other building block, the larger one in fact, is Qoala's agent enablement platform. As explained in the beginning of the chapter, Qoala's strategy was never to only play in the bite-sized lifestyle product space but instead to use it to educate consumers and therefore support their agent distribution strategy.

However, lack of consumer education and financial literacy is only one challenge agents are facing. Another one is the overhead costs for agents which leads to an inefficient use of their time. Lunani explained that his team discovered "that agents were spending 70-80% of their time doing things which are not value adding like following up on whether a payment has been made, whether a policy has been quoted or issued, and so on. Those tasks are very repetitive and non-value adding."

According to Lunani, many people decide against a career as an insurance agent because they dread the administrative work that comes with it. It is just not an attractive career in a country with such low awareness and minimal support even though commissions are higher compared to markets like Malaysia and Thailand.

Qoala is on a mission to make becoming an insurance agent more attractive. Lunani believes in order to truly increase insurance penetration the country needs more agents. He explained that "Indonesia only has 35,000 General Insurance agents. India has about a million, so 35,000 is not going to cut it if you want to increase penetration in this market."

Lunani compares it to the success ride-hailing had in Indonesia. While taxis existed, at least in major cities in Indonesia, ride-hailing companies like Grab and Gojek made it more accessible by "enlarging the driver base to a completely different scale. And you could argue that public transportation is better for it."

With Qoala's agent enablement platform, Lunani and his team want to make the career of selling insurance more attractive by supporting agents in their day-to-day management and by giving them access to more insurers and a broader portfolio of products.

In Indonesia, individuals can only obtain an agent license which ties them to one insurer. Qoala, however, has developed a model that allows individuals to become independent advisors and to sell insurance from a range of different insurance providers while being supported in their administrative activities.

Qoala holds a broker license which allows them to work with multiple insurers. Agents as well as individuals new to insurance can join Qoala as an affiliate and become an independent advisor which, on their own, they would not be able to do.

Historically the regulator would only grant agent licenses to work with one insurer to make sure that agents know the details of the products they are selling. This made sense to ensure quality as, in the past, it was impossible for one person to understand the differences of each insurer and their products, appetite, underwriting requirements and inclusions and exclusions.

With Qoala's agent enablement platform, Lunani explained, "those elements of risk are getting taken care of by us. All that the independent advisor has to do is enter the details of what a person is looking for, and in the backend, the platform figures out what process to apply across different insurances."

This not only enables independent advisors to offer a wider range of products and providers, but also helps minimize human errors and allows advisors to focus on value adding tasks.

"The power of this long term would be that not only can you make existing agents more efficient in serving consumers with multiple products, but, if you're really successful, it could lead to more people becoming agents," Lunani shared.

Qoala is in the process of building one of the largest sales channels for insurance in Indonesia. Historically insurers have been very protective of their own sales force and preferred to be in control. The sales force is often the part of an insurer that gets the most attention. Large teams are busy planning sales competitions that promise exciting incentives. This strategy not only motivates existing agents but also attracts new recruits.

However, I believe that this practice is also one of the reasons why insurance has sometimes a bad reputation. Too often, the focus is only on the sale and not on selling the right product that a client actually needs. If insurers had more resources to focus on product design and less on entertaining their sales channels, we might see even more innovative insurance solutions.

"We're hoping to help insurers understand that there is a new form of distribution which can be much more efficient if it's higher scale. At the end of the day distribution is a scale business."

– Harshet Lunani
Co-Founder, Qoala

We have witnessed other industries changing their distribution strategy and increasing their focus on designing competitive products. Lunani explained that "today, if you launch a new phone brand, for example, you would not start shops of your own. You probably will put it on Amazon. I think insurance is behind the curve but that's effectively what's happening. Not all retailers were excited to join Amazon on day one, but it happened over time. We're hoping to help insurers understand that there is a new form of distribution which can be much more efficient if it's higher scale. At the end of the day distribution is a scale business."

Maybe the answer to Indonesia's penetration problem and its fragmented market is offering insurance products at scale in a manner similar to how other products are marketed, through a large sales force enabled by technology. That way, insurers can shift their focus to building innovative products that cater to a population as diverse and unique as Indonesia.

The other question is, would such a model work in more mature markets with clear industry leaders and multi-carrier agent structures? Qoala is out to answer this question and has expanded its operation to the more advanced insurance markets in Malaysia and Thailand in addition to entering the Vietnam market.

Foundations for The Future

- Insurance isn't top-of-mind for most people. Lifestyle micro-insurance solutions can be a gentle way to demonstrate the benefits of insurance.

- As an insurtech startup when working with an insurer, make sure to manage expectations and define boundaries within which the insurtech can operate independently.

- Technology enables agents to work smarter, make less errors and be more efficient so they can focus on value-adding tasks.

- Creating an industry-wide sales force at scale can benefit the entire market and make the quality of the product the differentiator and not the talent of an insurer's agents.

7. bolttech

The startup world is often portrayed as this tale of 20-year-old college kids who have started a multi-billion-dollar company out of their parents' garage. While this might have been the case for Steve Jobs and Steve Wozniak, the founders of Apple, or Bill Hewlett and David Packard, the founders of HP, the median age at which founders started what would become a billion-dollar business is actually 34.[24]

I believe that, in an industry as heavily regulated and crucial to the economy of a country as insurance, having deep industry knowledge and experience comes in handy. Especially if it is experience gained during a crisis that revealed the weaknesses of the financial services industry.

In September 2008, during the peak of the Global Financial Crisis (GFC), American International Group (AIG) was on the verge of collapse. The company held the title of the world's largest supplier of traditional insurance at the time, and millions relied on it to safeguard their life savings. Additionally, AIG had a significant presence in several crucial financial markets, including municipal bonds. If AIG were to fail, it would have had a catastrophic impact on the stability of the broader economy and global financial markets. Consequently, the US Federal Reserve and Treasury intervened to prevent AIG from collapsing.[25]

Someone who witnessed this crisis and its impact on AIG firsthand is Rob Schimek. The lessons he learned throughout his career and especially from being at the center of the GFC helped Schimek and his team build one of the fastest growing insurtechs globally, bolttech. The company's incubation phase began in 2018 with the development of

---

[24] Scipioni, Jade, "This is the median age of billion dollar start-up founders, according to new research," *CNBC Make It*, 19 June 2023.
[25] "Investment in American International Group (AIG)," U.S. Department of the Treasury, 19 June 2023.

greenfield insurtech initiatives focused on digital insurance products and technology platforms for insurance distribution. Strategic acquisitions of smaller technology and insurance businesses – such as AmTrust Mobile Solutions Asia; i-surance in Europe; Axle Asia in Indonesia and AVA in Singapore – helped both to bring in new licenses and scale the business operations for the group. The brand launched officially to market in 2020 and the following year, achieved unicorn status with the largest Series A funding round (US$247 million) for an insurtech in history to date.

While we have seen larger funding rounds in recent years, they have been made into later stage insurtechs. In 2022, German startup Wefox, for example, secured US$400 million for its Series D round.[26] Series A, however, implies that a startup is still at the very beginning of its journey and venture capital provided is mainly used to set up initial operation and basic production to enable product development, marketing, and sales. It takes an industry veteran and the right setup to give investors enough confidence to participate in such a record-breaking Series A funding round.

Schimek's career includes decades of experience in the insurance industry. He spent 18 years with Deloitte & Touche in the United States, mostly serving financial institutions, and in particular, insurance companies. One of his main clients was MetLife, which he helped become a public company in 2000.

Schimek left Deloitte in 2005 and joined AIG. As the Chief Financial Officer of their global general insurance business, he navigated the company through the global financial crisis before becoming the global CEO of AIG's commercial insurance business in 2015. Schimek recalled "I learned so many things that I really admired in the way AIG had solved industry problems. But I probably learned equally as many things that I wouldn't want to replicate if I were starting all over."

Schimek left AIG at the end of 2017, and in early 2018, was appointed Managing Director and Group Chief Operating Officer of the life insurance group FWD, part of Asia-based Pacific Century Group (PCG). After founding FWD in 2013, PCG ventured into the

---

[26] "What were the biggest InsurTech deals of 2022?" Fintech Global, 20 June 2023.

P&C space by investing as an original shareholder in an insurtech startup several years later, with Schimek at the helm.

Schimek had the opportunity to start on a blank sheet, replicate everything he believed worked well within AIG and reinvent the parts that weren't working for the traditional insurance industry. What he built was called bolttech.

Schimek began to develop the strategic direction for bolttech shortly after his relocation to Asia in August 2018. "What an amazing journey since then. We took this company sort of out of nowhere from the beginning of 2019 and by 2021, we had a unicorn, completing the largest Series A in the history of the world for an insurtech" Schimek shared.

With a focus on general insurance, bolttech today is generating most of its revenue from its distribution capabilities.

Schimek took the lessons he had learned during his time working with and for the large insurers when designing the business model for bolttech. He shared, "I learned the power of choice. I learned the true potential of this general insurance space. I learned the value of a global organization that could serve needs, not just in one country, but across the world."

> "I learned the value of a global organization that could serve needs, not just in one country, but across the world."
>
> – Rob Schimek
> Group CEO, bolttech

To be able to operate globally, bolttech has a diverse set of capabilities, including different insurance licenses. In the US, bolttech is a licensed insurance distributor in all 50 states. In Europe and Asia, the group is licensed as an insurance distributor in most markets. This enables bolttech to meet the regulatory requirements to set up business in countries across the globe. In addition, the group also holds an underwriting license in Hong Kong under their general insurance business, bolttech Insurance.

However, what Schimek also learned was that he did not need to have all risks on his own balance sheet. Melissa Wong, bolttech's Group Chief Product Officer, believes that "it's almost impossible to be able to understand every risk and therefore having one player that is trying to provide every insurance product is not going to happen. So the idea was how can we bring different insurance players together to do better for the customer? And that cooperation, or coopetition, is really important because through technology we're understanding customer needs first, and then we're bringing different solutions together in one seamless journey."

Today bolttech operates as a technology-enabled ecosystem mainly in the B2B2C space. Bolttech's technology platform, which is known as an insurance exchange platform, connects buyers and sellers of insurance and allows insurance to be embedded in a contextual way with other products and services.

Embedded insurance has been one of the buzzwords of 2022 and many wonder what the hype is all about. Bryan Falchuk explained in his paper, "The Future of Auto Insurance: Connected, Embedded, Subscribed," that "some view embedded insurance as just another name for affinity marketing, but it goes far beyond that."[27]

Embedded insurance is about bundling an insurance offering with another product in a meaningful way. While we have had travel insurance embedded into travel booking sites for many years, what is different today is:

1. Expansion into new verticals
2. Tailor-made product offerings that are contextual to the core product being covered
3. Creating up-sell and cross-sell opportunities

To capture the value of embedded insurance, bolttech has three main use cases for its insurance exchange. The first one is working with licensed insurers that want to embed their products with a distribution or affinity partner. Many insurers lack the technology to integrate especially with digital platforms. Bolttech can help those insurers integrate with a partner and establish a new distribution channel.

The second use case is helping insurers that see potential in offering additional products to their client base but do not want to add such products to their own balance sheet. Schimek explained, "If you are well known as an auto insurer, but you want to offer a product other than auto insurance, we can do that for you. We bring homeowners insurance alongside the auto insurance offering and you're able to have an auto and home bundled product. Even though the auto insurance might be on our partner's balance sheet and the homeowner's

---

[27] Falchuk, Bryan, "The Future of Auto Insurance: Connected, Embedded, Subscribed," Insurance Evolution Partners, Boston, April 2022.

insurance might be on someone else's balance sheet, we help make that happen."

For some, this might be a radical new concept. An insurer selling not only their own products but products from other insurers to provide their customers more choice is foreign to many carriers. In my experience, insurers have generally had a mindset that demands full control of the product offering with no outsider interference. However, the rise of InsurTech has paved the way for more collaboration. Insurtechs have demonstrated how strategic partnerships and collaboration can create win-win situations for all parties involved which has led to more insurers being open to partnerships.

The third use case for bolttech, and the one we focus on in this chapter, is working directly with affinity partners that do not come from the insurance industry. These partners are often digital ecosystem platforms, meaning D2C platforms that digitally connect consumers to product and service offerings. Bolttech went a step further after noticing major differences in digital adoption and maturity between countries as well as industries. Given this, they support in-person distribution journeys, recognizing that some markets still value the human experience.

Bolttech focuses on partnerships mainly in five areas:
1. The telecommunication industry, where, for example, bolttech has established a commercial partnership embedding device protection with telecommunication provider AIS in Thailand.
2. Electronics Companies like Samsung;
3. Financial Services, and in particular non-banking finance companies, such as Home Credit;
4. Retail and e-commerce with companies like Lazada;
5. Super Apps like Maya in the Philippines or Rabbit Line Pay in Thailand.

Embedded insurance as a trend is not only driven by the insurance sector. In recent years we have witnessed more and more industries starting to offer insurance products. One of the reasons for adding insurance to the mix is to increase the average revenue per user (ARPU) as well as increasing loyalty and customer lifetime value through increased share of wallet.

Digitization has impacted and even disrupted many industries and their revenue models. If we look at the telecommunication space for example, this industry had to reinvent itself and find new revenue models repeatedly with the advent of the internet, mobile phones, texting, the transition away from landlines, mobile internet access and more.

Today, we hardly find traditional telecommunication revenue models like those we found with landlines anymore and even traditional mobile phone calls are on decline thanks to OTT (Over The Top) providers such as WhatsApp or LINE. The challenge for telecommunication providers, or telcos, is that OTT applications do not directly contribute to the operators' revenue yet use the providers' infrastructure to offer their services. Therefore, telcos globally are looking for new value-added services to leverage their often-large user base and increase revenue. Schimek shared that from partnerships with telcos and original equipment manufacturers (OEM) in Asia, bolttech expects omni-channel conversion rates of around 20-60%.

According to a report on embedded insurance published by the Coverager in 2022, the average conversion rate of AppleCare+ is 20-40% when offered in a brick-and-mortar store but only around 2.86% when offered online.[28]

To reach such comparably high conversion rates, not only is having the right product crucial, but also a frictionless user journey. Together with its partners, bolttech identifies ways insurance offerings can be embedded in a meaningful and contextual way into the partners' product offering and sales process. The challenge often is that the partner has no or very limited experience with the sale of insurance products and needs support to design the sales journey online as well as offline.

Even though bolttech operates globally with a range of different providers in different sectors, the team realized that there is no one-size-fits-all answer. For each country and each industry vertical, they think about the value proposition and conduct research with the individual partner on their specific client needs before launching a product.

---

[28] "Embedded Insurance: The Art and Science of Unselling Insurance," *Coverager*, 27 April 2023.

Unless a partner already has quality insights available on what their users or clients are looking for, a dedicated team from bolttech will come in and conduct primary research, often by gaining access to their partner's user base in addition to the general market research the insurtech conducts.

It is important to point out that, as the connector between supply and demand, bolttech not only thinks about the actual insurance product, but the packaging with other services as well as the entire user journey. Wong shared, "There's so much in the models around the product. How do you sell it? Is it an opt-in or opt-out? Is it a bundled product? Is it just one coverage option of a broader product? Is it a standalone product?" The team at bolttech looks at all these aspects and considers this holistic view as the value they bring to their partners.

One of bolttech's most popular products in the telecommunications space is their device protection offering. The team developed a product that exists at the intersection of service and insurance and gives customers more choice when selecting their device.

In some ways, smartphone protection is almost like the new motor insurance – an entry-level product to acquire new customers to then up-sell and cross-sell other products. More insurers might want to consider this space as we are already seeing first signs of a disruption of the motor insurance market globally.

"How do we make sure to capture the next opportunity to sell an embedded insurance product that makes sense to that person at that point in time."

– Melissa Wong
Group Chief Product Officer, bolttech

However, enabling ways to up-sell and cross-sell other products isn't as straight forward, especially in a digital sales channel without any agents or brokers to build a relationship with the client. Identifying a meaningful entry product is therefore just the first step. The next step is retaining the customer and creating tailor-made up-sell and cross-sell opportunities.

Wong shared that, "you can't just sell one device protection product and then switch across to travel insurance. That doesn't make any contextual sense for the customer. Therefore, we're constantly thinking, how do we make sure to capture the next opportunity to sell an embedded insurance product that makes sense to that person at that point in time."

The team at bolttech learned first-hand the importance of a product being contextual and adjacent. During the global pandemic, bolttech experimented with some of its retail partners to offer a COVID-19 cover to users and clients that had previously purchased device protection. COVID-19 was after all on everybody's mind so the team thought it would be an easy sell. However, it was not.

Wong recalled, "We weren't even able to give it away. And there were so many reasons for this. Cultural considerations, the feeling that it's too good to be true. So I think we've learned over the years of doing so many trials and tests that you can't just leap from A all the way to Z. You have to go through the steps. You have to work with your partner. You have to teach your partner to sell insurance. You have to even educate their consumer base about protection over a period of time."

Distribution in many ways is bolttech's core competency in addition to product design. When working with a partner, the insurtech sends what it calls 'ambassadors' to work within a partner's organization to help design and later tweak the sales process. Those ambassadors are often with a partner monthly, providing hands-on help optimizing the sales process. Wong explained that this is key to their success. "It's not natural for any of these partners to sell insurance or protection. They're really good at selling their own products, but they're not used to talking about protection and what makes it compelling for end consumers. So we spend a lot of time doing that. We have a whole team focused on this."

Once the first product has successfully been introduced into the partners offering, the team at bolttech together with their partner looks at the next stage. After all the goal is not to only sell one product, but to generate up-sell and cross-sell opportunities, as well as to increase customer stickiness and loyalty for the partner.

Additional coverages need to be connected or contextual to the entry product to do this. In the case of smartphone protection, bolttech developed a new type of subscription model that telcos can offer their clients.

The initial product concept allowed the telco customers, who had signed up for this add-on, to switch their phone to a comparable model or different color free of charge within a specified time period. While this product was very successful with customers as it gave them more choice and flexibility, the partner provided feedback that it wanted to increase customer stickiness.

A great reminder to not solely focus on a product's sales performance but also to assess its contribution to the broader, long-term strategy and comprehend the necessity of progressing a product to its subsequent phase. In our rapidly evolving world, successful entities shouldn't merely rest on their achievements, but rather plan and strategize for the future.

In the case of bolttech's telco partnerships, the team came up with an advanced version of the switch product that would also allow upgrades. With this product, customers were able to upgrade their old phone for a new model after 12 months in a seamless digital experience.

While the initial product only locked in a customer anywhere between 24 to 30 months, the new proposition keeps renewing every time a client upgrades to a new phone driving longevity and stickiness.

At its core, this type of subscription is not an insurance product but has an insurance protection component included. In order to get upgraded to the new model, the customer has to hand in their old phone. The business case for this product is based on the assumption that the old phone will be refurbished and therefore it still needs to be working. The insurance device protection component makes this possible.

Thinking about a product not only from an insurance lens but taking into account other services, the distribution mechanism and how insurance can complement a product to attract and retain more customers for their partner is the value proposition the bolttech team brings into a partnership.

In many cases, their products are designed in a way that consumers are unaware that it has an insurance component. They mostly perceive it as an additional service provided by their telco provider. This certainly is an evolution from the first embedded travel insurance products we saw in the market.

To enable the insurtech to come up with holistic products and services that don't center around insurance, bolttech has a combination of tech talents, entrepreneurs and seasoned industry professionals in their leadership team. According to Wong, this mix fuels bolttech's capacity to develop innovative embedded insurance solutions. The ingrained entrepreneurial ethos within bolttech's DNA enables the company to approach problem statements with fresh perspectives, and not have a solution already in the back of their minds.

Wong shared that "a lot of the big telcos, the big corporates, the banks, they've all had insurance pitching at them constantly. So how do you actually change the game a little bit? It's listen, listen, listen, and do a needs analysis properly, and then bring the minds together to try and figure out how to solve for their customers' needs. And the insurance component comes with that, as opposed to be starting with insurance."

Hence, it's not just about the entrepreneurial spirit; in-depth knowledge of insurance is crucial at the next stage to comprehend how it can be integrated. Many insurance elements required for a product, such as the telco device upgrade proposition, aren't readily available in the market. As a result, bolttech must collaborate with an entire insurance and service ecosystem to design these coverages or extract specific components from an existing stand-alone product.

Collaborating on such product ideas with established insurers can be challenging for many reasons. For example, the insurer's internal team may lack the experience to shift their perspectives when engaging with partners outside the insurance sector. This is particularly true for actuarial teams, which might not be adept at approaching product design from the perspective of an affiliate partner rather than from an insurance-centric viewpoint. After all, these highly qualified professionals often spend their entire careers in insurance and have little to no exposure to other industries.

This is just one of many reasons why it can be challenging working with external insurance partners on new product designs. However, even though bolttech has underwriting capabilities in Hong Kong as a registered licensed general insurer, the insurtech chooses to partner with other insurers on the supply side worldwide. Schimek explained that he "intends to keep bolttech as a balance sheet light, truly insurtech business, and not to recreate large, already very capable, general insurance players."

Rather than attempting to disrupt established insurers, bolttech acknowledges their expertise and fosters collaborations where each party contributes their individual strengths. The way bolttech was setup uniquely equips the insurtech to take leadership in such partnerships. Having underwriting capabilities and an experienced insurance team helps the young insurtech to talk to established insurers at eye-level and address any concerns at their end.

Wong explained that bolttech "can help insurers think about their products differently. In some cases, we can help them to customize the products because we understand insurance, as well. Unlike some pure-technology plays, we understand the risk side, so we can help them and bring them opportunities."

Looking at the product discovery and development process end-to-end, it typically starts with bolttech's research team identifying new opportunities with an affinity partner. After the research team has identified how a product or service should look like, they work together with the insurance experts within bolttech to identify what the insurance component should include before involving any insurance partners to develop and provide the actual insurance component.

While bolttech initially had to search for insurers that were willing to supply the insurance product, today they have a range of selected insurance partners that provide the underwriting component. This has the advantage that both teams, the one from bolttech and the one from the insurance partner, are already accustomed to working together, which removes friction and can speed up the process.

Streamlining processes and bolstering partnerships are crucial for any new entrant aiming for swift global expansion. Over the past three years, bolttech has established the requisite internal structure, placing a strong emphasis on nurturing successful partnerships, whether with affinity partners or underwriters.

The insurtech has developed a learning culture that systematically gathers feedback from partners to enhance both relationships and products and services. Every quarter, a bolttech team distributes surveys among different stakeholders at the partner's organization, evaluating their overall customer experience as well as that of their clients. The survey recipients range from C-level executives to product and frontline teams.

The survey results yield a score akin to a net promoter score (NPS), which, along with the partner's feedback, is reviewed quarterly by bolttech's leadership team. The responsible leaders within bolttech are then required to take action and respond to the partner's feedback. Wong explained "The team religiously pushes us to ensure that we've done something about the individual client feedback. And then obviously, our goal is to improve the overarching score across each of the accounts as well."

While recognizing the unique needs of different markets and collecting individual partner feedback, bolttech also concentrates on identifying synergies alongside modular technology that allows it to scale quickly. Wong, for example, heads a centralized product team that serves all verticals and markets globally, with specialists in specific verticals or regions offering support. These experts are the ones that match new partner opportunities with existing offerings or kickstart new product development.

Since its official launch in 2020, bolttech has constructed an internal structure that accommodates fast growth while constantly integrating new learnings. Globally, as of May 2023, bolttech's ecosystem connects over 700 distribution partners with more than 230 insurance providers and offers in excess of 6,000 product variations.

For me, bolttech is the next stage in the evolution of insurtech. It's not a startup that was founded by an insurance newbie thinking they can disrupt a century old industry with some shiny new technology. It is also not overly insurance focused but looks at the bigger picture on how to make insurance more accessible and remove friction in alternative forms of distribution.

Schimek started bolttech from a greenfield, taking into account all that he had learned during his career. He and his team have delivered remarkable growth. In May 2023 bolttech announced its US$196 million Series B round at a US$ 1.6 billion valuation. Funding was secured from global insurance giants, with Japanese insurer Tokio Marine taking the lead, and life insurance leader MetLife participating in the round through its subsidiary MetLife Next Gen Ventures.

While many predicted 2023 to be a tough year for investment into insurtech, the latest investment in bolttech has proven that insurtech is *not* dead. It might have just reached the next level of maturity.

Foundations for The Future

- Successful embedded insurance needs a well-engineered product strategy that is contextual to the core product and targets customer needs rather than selling unrelated offerings simply because you have a captive customer. Finding contextual expansions of the initial embedding moment can allow for an ongoing customer relationship rather than a one-off embedded sale.

- You do not need to take all risks on your own balance sheet. Partnerships are a powerful way to expand, offer more choice and allow you to focus on what you do best.

- Insurtech has grown up and industry veterans have entered the space. It is no longer about disruption but how to improve the industry as a whole from inside.

8. PhonePe

India is one of the hottest insurtech markets and has one of the fastest-growing startup ecosystems globally. With 107 unicorn startups as of 2022, India places third in a global unicorn ranking behind the USA and China.[29]

One of those unicorns is PhonePe. Founded in December 2015, the company emerged as one of India's largest payment apps, enabling digital inclusion for consumers and merchants alike. In 2020, PhonePe secured US$700 million in primary capital at a post-money valuation of US$5.5 billion.

In 2023, PhonePe raised US$850 million from global investors including General Atlantic, Ribbit Capital and Walmart at a pre-money valuation of US$12 billion, thus joining India's decacorn club.

Mobile payments and digital wallets have been on the rise in India since the demonetization event of 2016 when the government announced that all 500- and 1,000-rupee notes were instantaneously voided in an attempt to clean out the black market's cash supply and counterfeit notes. The government issued new notes and people were able to exchange their old notes exclusively at banks. However, printing press constraints resulted in the banks not having enough of the newly issued banknotes to meet the demand to replace the old ones, creating a cash crunch in the country.[30]

Demonetization and the problems around liquidity sparked the rise of digital payment systems in India. While it coincided with the adoption of digital payment tools like Apple Pay, Venmo and others

---

[29] "List of 107 Unicorn Startups in India and Counting | 2022 Updated," Startup Talky, 21 October 2022.
[30] "Cash and the Economy: Evidence from India's Demonetization," The Quarterly Journal of Economics, Volume 135, Issue 1, February 2020, Pages 57–103, 10 March 2023.

in Western economies, the development of digital payments in India took a very different route.

According to the World Bank's Global Findex Database, in 2011 over 89% of adults owned a bank account in the US, while only 35% did in India.[31] The population in the US had been accustomed to the banking system and using card payments for a few decades by then and over 70% of people over age 15 held a debit card in 2011.[32]

India, however, rapidly caught up with the US. Arguably, this was accelerated by the demonetization event. The shortage of cash drove an increase in bank account ownership in the country. In just ten years penetration more than doubled to 78% of adults in India owning a bank account in 2021.[33]

However, ownership does not equate to usage, suggesting traditional banking behaviors of Indians did not change. The World Banks' Global Findex report found that "India has the highest share of people who have accounts but do not use them" and the top reason identified for why people are not using their bank accounts is the distance from a financial institution.[34]

In March 2023, the New York Times reported that "the value of instant digital transactions in India last year [in 2022] was far more than in the United States, Britain, Germany and France" combined.[35]

The secret sauce to this rapid adoption of digital transactions in India was widely due to the introduction of the public digital infrastructure – Unified Payments Interface (UPI). The National Payments Corporation of India launched UPI as a standard set of functions and capabilities digital payment providers could build from, ensuring interoperability, richness and consistent capabilities across platforms.

UPI combined with the demonetization event was the perfect springboard for digital payment platforms like PhonePe. Over 800 million Indians – more than 60% of the population – own a mobile

---

[31] "The Global Findex Database 2021," The World Bank, 22 October 2022.

[32] "USA: Percent people with debit cards", The Global Economy, as of 3 April 2023.

[33] The World Bank, 2022.

[34] The World Bank, 2022.

[35] Kumar, Hari and Mujib Mashal, "Where Digital Payments, Even for a 10-Cent Chai, Are Colossal in Scale," *The New York Times*, 3 April 2023.

phone[36] and are now able to access mobile payment solutions thanks to widespread 4G mobile data coverage and UPI. This largely solved the location issue as these wallets operate fully digitally and are now enabling consumers to use their mobile phones to make digital payments. Unlike in most Western countries, mobile payments are widely used even for small payments in India. In fact, nearly 50% classify as small or micro-payments.[37]

This is an example of how developing countries can leapfrog technology stages. Most Western countries moved from a cash society to a bank society, which can be considered semi-digital. India, on the other hand, jumped straight to digital mobile payments. It both caught up to the West and did so with its own twist to enable everyone to make most transactions happen without the need for customers to visit or engage with the banks. They can simply link their bank accounts with a third-party payment app (TPAP) like PhonePe to make payments digitally.

Hemant Gala, Head of Financial Services at PhonePe, shared that the company launched in 2015 and therefore was perfectly positioned to take advantage of the demonetization by offering its users mobile payments to overcome the cash shortage they suddenly faced.

UPI allowed PhonePe to build a secure and scalable digital payment system and using it helped build trust and made consumers feel comfortable using the PhonePe app to make payments. UPI was built by the National Payments Corporation of India (NPCI), a not-for-profit Indian financial services organization functioning under the Reserve Bank of India (RBI) and the Indian Banks' Association (IBA) to promote and facilitate the adoption of electronic payments in India. Gala explained "UPI stack was the first of its kind in the world – with a native, mobile-first, interoperable payment experience for consumers. Nowhere in the world did a platform like this exist."

Getting its app users to make payments was the first growth stage for PhonePe. Gala explained that sending money used to be very complex in India but UPI revolutionized sending money and enabled the transfer of payments in seconds over a mobile phone.

---

[36] Pachari, Smita, "Demonetization: Unpacking the Digital Wallets," *We Ken-International Journal of Basic and Applied Sciences*, December 2016.
[37] *The New York Times*, 3 April 2023.

After having solved the major pain points of sending money in India, the company turned to the aspects of spending money. Gala explained focusing on "spending money is about gaining ubiquity so that people get the confidence and have the opportunity to spend, wherever they go, if it is a department store, if it is a mall, if it's a small store, if it's a corner store, if it's a pharmacy or a grocery store, or if they are shopping online, they have the option to pay through PhonePe."

From the start, PhonePe had a vision to serve the whole financial services spectrum and not only payments. Therefore, after successfully introducing sending and spending money, PhonePe focused on the third phase in their strategy – manage and grow - which is "about helping people manage their life, their risks, their money, and helping them grow their money" as Gala explained.

From a long-term perspective, it's crucial to expand digital payments to financial services and help consumers navigate the whole spectrum, end-to-end. Building a solid userbase riding on payments helped build a sizeable scale of customers for PhonePe, however the payments business operates on razor-thin margins, hence it's the first step towards solving for financial services.

This is a reminder of how many years and how many millions of users it took Facebook, Spotify, Google, and others to establish a monetization model and reach profitability. Only when enough users have joined a platform and trust it, companies can introduce products that help them reach profitability and increase margins in the next stage.

While, according to Gala, PhonePe had a valid business model just focusing on payments, the company stuck to its vision of servicing the entire spectrum of financial services. The goal of the company is to "create real impact on financial inclusion in India," explained Gala. And he added, "even if one line of my business is profitable, I still want to invest in marketing; in growing the insurance business; the investment business. I'm growing new businesses continuously because we see a real opportunity to solve for financial inclusion."

After running the payment business for four years, PhonePe was well positioned to venture into new lines of business. Its users had gained confidence and trust in the company and PhonePe had successfully created a new habit among its users of using its app to make all kinds of small and large payments. Gala explained, "changing of habits needs a lot of convincing, education and a lot of effort on the ground with customers." Over the years, PhonePe had become part of the daily lives of its users, and it felt natural for them to turn to PhonePe for other financial services related needs.

"I'm growing new businesses continuously because we see a real opportunity to solve for financial inclusion."

– Hemant Gala
Head of Financial Services, PhonePe

Gala explained that PhonePe, "could have gone into insurance distribution in the first year of our journey but we identified two key elements to be successful that we needed before doing that. The first is to be very focused on doing what we're doing at a point in time and go very deep and scale it up. The second one is to wait until customers have enough trust in the platform before extending it."

Financial services products, including insurance, require a lot of trust from consumers. Without trust, consumers are unlikely to entrust their savings to a digital payments platform, let alone making basic daily transactions with it.

After being confident that they had the trust needed from their users, PhonePe launched its first insurance product in January 2020. In addition to expanding their offering to advanced financial services to users and therefore the opportunity to increase loyalty, it also meant new revenue streams and the chance to generate higher margins.

Launching the insurance vertical meant the team had to identify which product to start with and find the right partner to work with. In 2019, PhonePe had acquired a corporate agent license, which allowed them to work with up to three general insurers, three life insurers and three health insurers.

Launching a new vertical can be an intense period for everyone involved. The future of the new team often depends on the success of the first product. Keeping in mind that insurance in general is considered to be a push product and that PhonePe had plans to sell it exclusively through their app and in a market with low financial literacy, identifying the right insurance product was important.

Some market research that the team at PhonePe had conducted showed that 30-35% of travel insurance products were already purchased digitally – a trend we have been witnessing worldwide for over a decade now. Travel insurance can be considered one of the first insurance products that has successfully been embedded in online platforms, so it is not surprising that the team at PhonePe considered it a safe bet to launch their insurance vertical with.

However, identifying the right product is only the first step, the next, and arguably the more important step is finding the right insurance carrier to partner with.

PhonePe's vision was not to replicate an existing product offering but to fully integrate a travel insurance product into its mobile app in a meaningful way that allowed even first-time users to buy insurance with ease. Overall, PhonePe has a strong focus on customer centricity and simplifying the user journey. As a digital payment app that is focused on bringing financial services to the previously unbanked, PhonePe spends a lot of attention on simplifying the user journey, so it is intuitive for any user.

This meant rethinking some of the existing traditional sales processes and adjusting the user journey, so it matched the overall standard PhonePe had developed for its other services.

The fintech partnered with multiple insurance companies in India that had identified great potential in digital partnerships and new-age distribution models. Moreover, these insurers were willing to adjust their processes and to work with the team at PhonePe to optimize the user journey.

Gala shared that the insurers created "almost like a SWAT team" that was interacting with the team at PhonePe on a daily level to build out new APIs in order to integrate the new insurance offering into the PhonePe app.

However, more challenging than the technical integration were the legal aspects. When selling insurance products from third-party carriers, the terms and conditions of the insurers must be included, and any inclusions and exclusions must be explained. This can be very complex and confusing especially for first-time buyers of insurance.

To be able to simplify the user journey and make the sales process easier to understand in a completely digital setup, the team at PhonePe had to break down the entire process including the terms and conditions (T&Cs) of the insurance itself.

Insurance is a highly regulated industry with complex requirements and strict data privacy laws guarded by legal and compliance teams within every insurance company. For many carriers, those responsible for compliance are often more focused on playing it safe than finding the best solution for the customer given that their job is to ensure the organization stays out of regulatory trouble. This is understandable as high fines or other penalties can result from breaching regulations, but it does not always lead to ideal customer experiences.

However, a strict regulatory environment was nothing new to PhonePe. Starting as a digital payment company meant that, from day one, the fintech had to play within the rules outlined by the regulators and had to deeply understand the nuances of the law. When starting the insurance vertical, Gala shared that the team studied every single clause within every single guideline of the regulation.

PhonePe worked closely with horizontal functions of their insurance partners including product development, underwriting, pricing and especially compliance and legal. The teams debated the interpretation of regulations, guidelines, and clauses, and analyzed what information was mandatory for the issuance of a policy and which was just nice to have. This is what led the partners to break away from their legacy approach and convinced them to adjust their APIs to a new and simpler user journey.

What is impressive is that a team with limited insurance knowledge was able to challenge incumbent insurers to change their views and interpretation of the regulation. While the top management of the insurance division at the time had deep insurance knowledge, the rest of the team did not. It is a great example of how an outsider with fresh eyes is sometimes best suited to successfully challenge the *status quo*.

What made the team at PhonePe successful was their Product Oriented Delivery (POD) structure, where various functional stakeholders sat down together to try to achieve a common ambition. POD is a model that is often used in software development and is centered on building small, self-sufficient cross-functional teams that have the skills to design, develop, test, and operate a product.

Within a POD, information flow is extremely fast and extremely transparent. Therefore, things usually get done a lot quicker because most people are on the same page regarding the objectives and components required to meet that objective.

It took Gala and his team six months of intensive project work, but on 26th of January 2020 they launched the first insurance product on the PhonePe platform.

This was a huge win for the young team; however, they barely got a chance to celebrate as only a few weeks later COVID-19 hit, bringing travel to a near-complete standstill in India and globally. Obviously, that had immediate implications for the young insurance business at PhonePe since the market for their sole product essentially evaporated overnight.

> "This really built our confidence that, as a team, we were able to turn around our learnings on the travel product and quickly bring together an offering which was really relevant at that moment in time."
>
> – Hemant Gala
> Head of Financial Services, PhonePe

While COVID-19 was a black swan event, an extreme rarity with a significant impact globally, setbacks are part of doing business, especially when trying something new. What differentiates successful companies is the motivation of their teams to not give up, to leverage what they have learned, and apply it to the next opportunity.

When COVID-19 was declared a global pandemic, the team at PhonePe recognized the opportunity to launch a new health insurance product. Gala recalled, "we realized there is no single Corona virus specific health insurance offering available in the market today that is completely online."

Leveraging on the lessons learned from the previous project, the teams at PhonePe and at the insurance partners from the travel product moved quickly and within just two and a half weeks received regulatory approval and launched a new COVID-19 product on the PhonePe app.

This was a huge achievement for the team and obviously a much-needed product in the Indian market. Demand was extremely strong, making it a pull rather than a push product, unlike the typical way insurance has been sold in the Indian market so far. Gala shared, "This really built our confidence that, as a team, we were able to turn around our learnings on the travel product and quickly bring together an offering which was really relevant at that moment in time."

What is remarkable about this example is the fact that PhonePe managed to attract people that have never interacted with an insurance provider before. According to a survey the team at PhonePe conducted, 60-65% of users that bought the COVID-19 cover were first-time insurance buyers. "Even though they were new insurance buyers, when you put a product in front of people in a clear and simple customer journey, they understood what they needed and were able to buy it," Gala shared.

In terms of the overall company strategy of PhonePe, this was a big success as well. The team had proven that they were able to successfully launch an insurance product on the digital payment app that could generate top-line revenue.

However, while this was a success worth celebrating, they had an advantage in being one of the first movers in India during a major global crisis, offering a product that was on everyone's mind. The question was, could PhonePe replicate the success with more traditional insurance products that would lead to a steady, long-term revenue stream?

Many argue that not all insurance products are suitable to be sold online as a pull product. While apps like PhonePe have the capability to push marketing messaging about a product to their users, it is not the same as having a conversation with an agent or a broker that is explaining the benefits of insurance.

At PhonePe, Gala and his team wanted to focus on specific use cases that made sense in the Indian market and were mostly self-explanatory to their users. They came across a study that showed that roughly 57% of two-wheelers in India are uninsured. This is mainly because most vehicle insurance is sold at the dealership when the vehicle is purchased, but renewal rates drop off after the first year, and only go down from there.

With their insurance partners, PhonePe once again managed to break down the complex onboarding journey into a few easy steps. What used to be a multi-page application is now less-than-a-minute digital buying journey for consumers. In addition, PhonePe leverages its existing customer data to pre-fill some of the KYC information required, shortening the journey further.

To successfully sell insurance direct-to-consumers via a mobile application, it is crucial to minimize the information that needs to be entered. Reading long and complex paragraphs on a small screen also does not make for a great user experience. This is only exacerbated when users have lower levels of financial literacy.

PhonePe's market penetration is higher in tier II (population in the range of 50,000 to 100,0000) and tier III cities (population in the range of 20,000 to 50,000). Those cities are often characterized by a large population of consumers who are relatively new to buying insurance. Their success selling their COVID-19 coverage was also primarily with people who have never bought insurance before. As a result, the buying and onboarding process they designed had to be as simple as possible.

It is debatable if the platform brand, in this case, PhonePe, and a well-designed user journey are more important or the range of insurance brands that are offered on the platform. In other words, do consumers care only about the product or also about the brand and reputation of the insurance carrier?

After successfully launching its two-wheeler insurance in October 2020, the team at PhonePe started to realize that they were losing a considerable amount of potential insurance customers as their users were missing choice.

PhonePe conducts surveys on a regular basis to learn first-hand about their customer's user experience. The survey results showed that users felt there was a lack of choice, especially of some of the major insurance brands they had an affinity to. "We realized the need to play on the brand affinity of large insurance companies because PhonePe was not yet an established insurance distributor," Gala explained. The survey revealed that users did not feel confident that PhonePe would provide them with the best product as they had no way of comparing different products from different providers.

Based on this feedback, PhonePe embarked on a journey to become a one-stop-shop where users can find any product from any insurer that is available in the market, so their users do not need to go anywhere else to compare products and have more confidence in PhonePe as all major brands trust the company enough to allow them to offer their products.

This meant PhonePe had to make changes to their license. The company held a corporate agent license which only allowed them to work with a limited number of insurers. In August 2021, PhonePe acquired an insurance broker license and went from working with three motor insurers to roughly 10 insurers in the span of a month.

Gala shared that they immediately felt the impact of this decision, confirming their survey findings that the limited choice of insurers was impacting their sales and therefore bottom line.

"The number of quotes and policies being sold just exploded," Gala recalled, and this is where he and the team understood that while it is important to find the right product and design a user-friendly journey, the brand of the insurer and the illusion of choice does matter to consumers. There are people out there who want to buy insurance themselves, but they want to feel like they are in control of their choice and get the best deal available in the market.

To onboard a range of different insurers, however, isn't an easy task. The team at PhonePe was talking to 10-12 insurers simultaneously and, the majority had a certain way of doing things. It took the team a while to convince the carriers that certain things are not really required from a regulatory standpoint, or even an underwriting standpoint.

What again made PhonePe successful was the work they put into really understanding what the law explicitly required and what it did not. The team had long and honest conversations with the compliance and legal teams of their insurance partners to jointly discuss how to interpret laws and regulations with the goal of identifying the best solution possible for the customer that would make the journey simpler and easier to understand.

In the end, both PhonePe and their insurance partners benefitted from this process. Many insurers went back and started making those same changes to their own digital journeys on their websites. "They probably hadn't looked at it from a mobile-first journey," Gala shared.

After PhonePe had proven with several insurance partners that their model works on a mobile-only destination, more insurers felt comfortable joining the platform and were open to following PhonePe's suggestions to improve and simplify the customer journey.

Streamlining the sales process is not only important from a user journey perspective but also to ensure efficiencies. Against what many had hoped when digital sales channels first entered the market, selling digitally has not led to a reduction in distribution costs, but has instead created a price war in many markets around the world.

Gala, who had started his career in the insurance industry, understands well the struggles and challenges of selling online. With

PhonePe, he aims for insurers to build an additional distribution channel that is profitable and sustainable.

For example, while any digital sales journey aims to reduce the number of datapoints that need to be collected for a quote, the team at PhonePe understands the importance of some of those datapoints for the healthy underwriting of a portfolio and works with insurers to find the optimal balance.

In a relatively short period of time, PhonePe Insurance Broking Services emerged as one of the fastest-growing insurtech distributors in the country, selling over 5.9 million policies as of the end of July 2023.

While PhonePe benefits from the range of well-known brands and the choice they provide users, their insurance partners benefit from the insights PhonePe can generate from its large user-base.

As of July 2023, PhonePe had 5.5 billion transactions per month across over 480 million registered users and over 220 million monthly active users.

Some of the data, insights and trends PhonePe is generating from its large user base is available to the public via PhonePe Pulse, India's first interactive website on digital payments in the country. The platform offers rich insights into how digital payment adoption has evolved across India and includes detailed geographical and category-specific trends. For example, PhonePe Pulse data shows that, for Q4 2022, the Indian state of Maharashtra ranked as the number one market with over 1.8 million insurance sold through PhonePe, with a total premium value of INR 180 million (~US$2.2 million).

In addition to the publicly available PhonePe Pulse data, PhonePe builds propensity models to understand what type of product to push to which category of user and shares these insights with its insurance partners. PhonePe advises them about the demographics of the customer base and how they can make adjustments to sell more across different demographics.

In addition, PhonePe leverages some of the technologies that had initially been developed for the payment side of the business. For example, the fraud risk detection algorithm it developed can be used for the insurance vertical as well.

PhonePe's insurance business is still relatively at the beginning of its journey, and so is India. In 2020, insurance penetration was at just

4.2% compared to 12.5% in the US and 10.8% in Singapore.[38] The country has huge potential and is on its way to becoming a leading insurtech nation globally and PhonePe has grown to become one of India's largest digital insurance distributors in the last two years.

We have seen a range of US companies invest into fintechs and insurtechs in India. While Walmart invested in PhonePe, Amazon invested in neo insurer Acko,[39] and MassMutual Ventures invested in distribution insurtech Turtlemint,[40] to name just a few. With its large, underinsured population, the growth potential is certainly one reason for the global interest in India's insurance industry.

"There almost couldn't be a better time to work on building a digital-first insurance distribution business."

*– Hemant Gala
Head of Financial
Services, PhonePe*

Gala explained why he thinks the Indian market is unique. "I started my career two decades ago in insurance when the Indian insurance market opened up to private players. Today we have come a long way, India is flourishing with many more players across all lines of the insurance business both General Insurance and Life & Health. There is a very enabling regulatory environment and policymakers have a very strong intent to drive insurance penetration. There almost couldn't be a better time to work on building a digital-first insurance distribution business. Just like in payments, India will be the source for a lot more innovations on product and technology for insurance in the coming years."

---

[38] "Insurance indicators: Penetration," OECD Stats, 25 April 2023.
[39] "Acko," Crunchbase, 06 October 2022.
[40] "Turtlemint," Crunchbase, 06 October 2022.

Foundations for The Future

- In order to break down processes to meet modern customer expectations, you need to start with regulation first to understand the very essence of the law.

- Insurance can be sold online as a pull product if the setup is right. This means having the right product, a well-engineered user journey and making consumers feel like they are in control.

- Developing markets don't necessarily follow the same path as developed markets but can allow players to leapfrog technology adoption stages. India is a market to watch and draw inspiration from even for more mature markets given what it has shown about digital distribution and the potential for insurance to be bought, not sold.

9. Ping An

In 2022, Ping An was ranked the second largest insurer globally based on net premiums written (NPW).[41] Ping An exceeded the third largest insurer, the global insurance group AXA, by over US$7.5 billion. An astonishing achievement for a comparatively young company.

AXA was founded in 1816, is present in 51 countries and serves 93 million clients globally.[42] AXA Tianping Property & Casualty Insurance Company Ltd is the largest 100% foreign-owned P&C insurer in the Chinese market.[43]

Ping An, on the other hand, was only founded in 1988 by Peter Ma, an exceptional entrepreneur, who is today the chairman of the company. Ping An was the first joint-stock P&C insurer in China. From the beginning, however, Ma had a vision to create a broader financial services company, a platform that offers a wide range of products and services.

In 2022, Ping An ranked 25th in the Fortune Global 500 list and fourth among global financial services companies. In their 2022 annual report, the company announced that its vision is to become a "World-leading Integrated Finance and Healthcare Services Provider." Ping An Group provides diverse products and services to over 227 million retail customers and over 647 million internet users.[44]

Ping An's story closely aligns with the story of modern-day China, explained Jonathan Larsen, the Chief Innovation Officer at Ping An Group and Chairman and Chief Executive Officer of its Global

---

[41] "World's Largest Insurance Companies (NPW) – 2022 Edition," *Best's Review,* A.M. Best Company, Oldwick, NJ, 2022.
[42] "About Us," AXA Group, Paris, France, as of 6 June 2023.
[43] "AXA has completed the acquisition of the remaining 50% stake in AXA Tianping," AXA Group, Paris, France, as of 6 June 2023.
[44] "2022 Annual Report," Ping An Insurance (Group) Company of China, Ltd., Shenzhen, China, 2022.

Voyager Fund. "In 1988, when Ping An started, there were hardly any privately owned cars in China. Today, Ping An is the largest car insurer in the world." Larsen pointed out.

Ping An excels in many lines of business. It is the largest life insurer and health insurer in China and their banking arm is doing more credit card volume in China than American Express or Citigroup does in their consumer lines globally.

> "In 1988, when Ping An started, there were hardly any privately owned cars in China. Today, Ping An is the largest car insurer in the world."
>
> – Jonathan Larsen, Chief Innovation Officer, Ping An Group

Ping An is a giant among giants and even outside of traditional financial institutions, in the FinTech and InsurTech space, the company plays a major role. Ping An's technology-empowered personal financial services platform, Lufax, is the largest non-bank lender in China and the Global Voyager Fund invests in insurtechs all over the world.

How did Ping An not only establish its insurance practice in the local Chinese market with fierce competition, but rose to be one of the largest financial services groups worldwide in an objectively short period of time? I believe some of the success factors are:

1. Their unique ecosystem approach,
2. A culture that embraces new technologies, and
3. The overall entrepreneurial spirit of the company.

To understand Ping An's journey to the top, it is worth looking at the company's history and the strategic decisions made. When Ping An first started, the company focused on building a solid insurance business. This included setting up internal operations and processes, acquiring the needed licenses, and building the knowledge and skills required to run a diverse insurance business. Insurance is a highly regulated industry across the globe and China is no exception. Getting the legal foundations right is crucial to building a sustainable insurance business and something many insurtechs today have struggled with.

From 2000 onward, Larsen shared how Ping An's focus began to shift. Having the necessary foundations in place, Ping An decided to move away from a product-centered strategy to a customer access strategy. "The idea was as much as possible, subject to the constraints of legal entity boundaries within the Chinese regulatory environment, to be able to provide as integrated a service offering as possible. And at the same time, Ping An decided to integrate their client database to allow a total view of every customer. And very importantly, Ping An was the first organization in China to introduce Net Promoter Score (NPS) measurement back in 2000."

Most insurers only started including NPS in their KPIs in the past 5-10 years. The fact that Ping An introduced this key indicator in the early 2000s is an example of the forward-thinking mindset and culture of the young insurance company. Early on, the company tried to have a holistic view of their customers and how they think about the company, making it one of the first insurers to adopt a truly customer centric strategy.

The trigger for Ping An's next major change in strategy came with the invention of the modern smartphone in 2007. Compared to the US and Europe, China was less impacted by the Global Financial Crisis and therefore had more bandwidth to explore new opportunities brought by the invention of the smartphone.

This was also the time the world witnessed the rise of Chinese technology giants including Baidu, Alibaba and Tencent (also referred to as "BAT"). These companies enjoyed dramatic growth and demonstrated a rapid leapfrogging from analog to mobile and digital technology.

According to Larsen, Ma understood early that a new economic model was emerging. He not only saw potential in digitizing retail and entertainment but predicted that digitization would have a large impact on the financial services industry. Ma believed that almost everything we do in finance can be digitized and that the boundaries between traditionally separate businesses will not only be blurred, but redefined or even erased.

The birth of the smartphone heralded a fundamental behavior change in many areas – most importantly, how consumers interact with various service and solution providers. Instead of seeing this as a threat to Ping An's existing business model, Ma saw an opportunity. Digital was going to allow business lines to be integrated in completely new ways. This resulted in the second major transformation in the company's young history when Ma pivoted Ping An to be a technology-first company.

Technology was viewed as an enabler that would allow Ping An to reshape the existing business so it could quickly respond to changes in customer behavior and embrace emerging digital business models. Between 2010 and 2016, the team at Ping An moved the entire company to the cloud, long before most insurers or other financial services firms even contemplated such moves, let alone completed them. "I think we're the only large financial institution that is basically entirely cloud-based today" explained Larsen.

Indeed, even today, very few insurance groups the size of Ping An have a holistic cloud strategy and managed to completely move to the cloud. Most major insurance incumbents are still heavily dependent on legacy technology, with on premises, legacy hardware and systems.

One of the major elements of this shift has been to systematically acquire talent to provide both the leadership and skillset required to operate. Ping An has recruited extensively in the tech industry across many disciplines, ranging from AI and machine learning, blockchain, agile development, API and microservice architecture, and cloud computing infrastructure management. "Hiring great people and allowing them to create new solutions within the Ping An environment has proven a very attractive value proposition. And of course, great people attract great people," Larsen says. As a consequence, Ping An has become something of a magnet for talent.

> "Hiring great people and allowing them to create new solutions within the Ping An environment has proven a very attractive value proposition. And of course, great people attract great people."
>
> – Jonathan Larsen
> Chief Innovation
> Officer, Ping An
> Group

Moving the entire IT infrastructure to the cloud also meant a reassessment and re-engineering of core processes – a challenge that should not be underestimated. While changing legacy technology is a time-consuming and costly endeavor, changing people's behavior and reengineering processes can be an even bigger challenge. It needs a culture that embraces change and the willingness of people to consequentially rethink and challenge the *status quo*.

Ma has endeavored to create a culture driven by ideas and vision, but always with a bias for action and delivery. "Debate is encouraged, but once a decision is made, we act as one. This is a key part of the culture," Larsen explained.

Notwithstanding the challenges, those projects are necessary to stay relevant. Digital has fundamentally changed the word and has blurred the lines of many industries. Technology giants have disrupted countless business models and redefined competition.

To give an example, Amazon started by selling books online in 1995 and is today the world's largest cloud computing provider.[45] Furthermore, Amazon today is not only one of the largest distributors of video content in the world, but one of the largest producers of video content, as well.

Before Amazon and before the digitization of the economy, all those businesses had been thought unrelated. A bookshop was never in direct competition with a video rental store and certainly not a movie studio. However, a single company disrupted them all and has not only entered a range of different industries but is dominating many of those businesses today while also creating completely new categories and markets.

What all those disrupted spaces have in common is that their business models were defined by their traditional distribution channels and the constraints inherent to them.

Amazon built a platform to sell online and even deliver some of those products digitally. As a first mover in many of those fields, Amazon developed the cloud technology needed to enable their business inhouse. However, instead of keeping the technology to themselves, they made the decision to capitalize on their technological capabilities by productizing and commercializing them, launching Amazon Web Services (AWS), their cloud computing business. AWS operates independently from other business units within Amazon and is an example of corporate venture building – when an established company builds a separate venture from scratch.[46]

We can find many similarities between Amazon and Ping An. Just like Amazon, Ping An has an appetite for innovation and launching new business ventures outside their core business.

One of the first digital business model ventures launched by Ping An was a health care software company. In 2014, Ping An founded

---

[45] Richter, Felix, "Amazon Leads US$180-Billion Cloud Market," Statista, 6 June, 2023.

[46] "Venture building as an innovation strategy," Board of Innovation, Antwerp, Belgium, 6 June 2023.

Ping An Healthcare and Technology Company Limited, also known as Ping An Good Doctor (Good Doctor). While Good Doctor does provide new business leads for Ping An's insurance business today, it was founded with the purpose of being a business model in and of itself.

Larsen explained that private healthcare is still at a very early stage in China. He shared that "less than 10% of health costs are covered by private insurance, but it's growing at 40% a year and is going to evolve to look very similar to health insurance in the private sector in other markets around the world."

However, Ping An's ambitions were not merely to enter this growing market but to reach beyond that and redefine the addressable market using digital technology following the strong belief that digital technology unlocks you from the constraints of your traditional business model and distribution channel.

Ping An's vision was to create a health care provider that is built as a technology company. In this way, it can reshape the entire private health care system and will be relevant not only to those using private health insurance, but to everyone in China.

What clearly sets Ping An apart from most large corporations, is the fact that they treat such endeavors not as an internal corporate project, but as a new entity with third party shareholders and investors, assembling a team of entrepreneurs who hold equity in the newly formed startup. Larsen explained, "From the beginning, we brought in third party shareholders and investors. We set it up as a standalone entity."

Starting a new tech startup requires very different skills than running an existing business. The entrepreneurial spirit is highly important and so is the understanding of new trends and evolving technologies. In the case of Good Doctor, most of the founding team had no experience in the insurance or healthcare industry but came from Chinese technology giant Alibaba with first-hand experience of building a digital platform.

Several insurers across the globe have launched corporate venture building projects. However, management from the insurance incumbent is often selected for key positions in the newly built ventures rather than bringing in outside talent. I believe this is one of the reasons we do not see many successful examples of corporate venture building projects. In addition to different skills needed, mindset and culture plays a major role and we often see a clash between corporate and startup culture. Furthermore, the strong ties to the incumbent can be a constraint that keeps the startup from thinking outside the box or being willing to attempt to disrupt the market.

In the case of Good Doctor, the founding team followed a holistic strategy that went beyond the current business model of Ping An. They did not focus on how to integrate insurance offerings but instead analyzed how to improve private healthcare service and address the countless pain points with technology used in healthcare delivery.

The primary healthcare system in China is often typified by long wait times for patients and low service quality. Good Doctor developed a service that allows the startup to offer simple consultations via digital channels and only send patients to see a doctor if absolutely necessary. This is not only faster with a better customer experience but also very cost effective at scale.

Good Doctor covers the first level of care and is primarily a text-based health care service. The startup operates with automated questions to understand and analyze the needs of the patient. Based on the symptoms, the user will be virtually connected with a doctor and is able to send text messages as well as photos and videos as needed.

If the doctor cannot make a diagnosis virtually or if the condition is too severe and the patient needs to see somebody physically, the online doctor can immediately make an appointment at a hospital or clinic.

In terms of prescribing pharmaceuticals, doctors on Good Doctor's virtual platform can issue certain prescriptions that are then delivered to the patient. For any pharmaceuticals they are not allowed to prescribe in a virtual consultation, they can arrange appointments to meet a physician in person who can prescribe what is needed.

Good Doctor is essentially a gateway to the health system that is not only more convenient, but in many cases more cost effective. However, a business model like this is only cost-effective when enough members use it, given the upfront investment needed to build the technology behind the solution and the high cost of customer acquisition for most direct-to-consumer models.

This is where the power of the Ping An Group came in. Ping An supported member acquisition for Good Doctor by leveraging its large life insurance agency force that served roughly 200 million financial services customers across the whole group at the time.

While Good Doctor was marketed through online channels, the majority of initial members came through the proprietary client base of Ping An agents. Ping An's 200 million customers were informed about this new digital health care offering by their agents, allowing the startup to scale quickly. This push gave Good Doctor rapid growth and instant scale, starting a flywheel effect on their growth that helped Good Doctor quickly become economically self-sustaining.

While initially Good Doctor benefitted from the client base of Ping An Group, today we see the reverse effect. Good Doctor acts as a lead generator for Ping An's financial products and allows the insurer to introduce new health insurance products to Good Doctors' user base. As of the end of 2021, Good Doctor had over 420 million registered users on its platform, while cumulative consultations neared 1.3 billion since launch.[47]

"Putting mediocre capabilities together and expecting value to arise is not going to happen. But if you can find the right way to connect them, it can be very powerful."

– Jonathan Larsen, Chief Innovation Officer, Ping An Group

Just like Amazon, Ping An Group aims to be excellent in each of its business ventures and not only sees them as supporting businesses for their core insurance business. Larsen explained "You still have to be excellent in each of these individual capabilities. Putting mediocre capabilities together and expecting value to arise is not going to happen. But if you can find the right way to connect them, it can be very powerful, both from a client perspective, as well as from a business model perspective."

In their 2022 annual report, Ping An stated that the group acquired 29.7 million new retail financial customers in 2022; over 35% of whom were sourced from its internet user base for the third consecutive year.[48] Furthermore, the company declared that customers who used services from the Group's internet ecosystems, including companies like Good Doctor, held 2.4 times more contracts and 5.9 times more

---

[47] "About Us," Ping An Insurance (Group) Company of China, Ltd., as of 6 June 2023.
[48] "2022 Annual Report," Ping An Insurance (Group) Company of China, Ltd., Shenzhen, China, 2022.

assets under management (AUM) per capita than those who did not use such services. Clearly, the ecosystem is driving highly attractive business into the group.

Larsen explained, that "if you make it convenient for customers to access your services online, particularly through mobile devices, then those customers tend to be much more loyal, much stickier than customers that have just bought one product with you and don't have this ongoing interaction."

However, just because a lead starts within one of the internet ecosystems, does not mean all insurance policies are sold straight through online. Larsen explained that depending on the product journey as well as the preference of the customer, there might be an offline component in the sales journey. For example, a lead coming from Good Doctor could be picked up by a Ping An insurance agent if the customer prefers to clarify open questions with a real person and not an AI chatbot before closing the contract.

Good Doctor is just one example of the many internet ecosystems Ping An has built or, in some cases, acquired. For example, Ping An acquired Autohome in 2016, an online one-stop-shop for all things cars. As an example of one it built, Ping An founded Lufax, which provides financing services to small and micro-business owners as well as wealth management solutions for the middle class.

Apart from client facing digital business models, Ping An also made strategic investments into companies that have developed a technology Ping An needed to run a truly digital financial services company as well as looking for opportunities to monetize the cutting-edge technology the group had developed in-house.

When Larsen joined Ping An in 2017, he set up the Global Voyager Fund. Ping An had decided to commit US$1 billion of capital to invest in digital health and fintech initiatives. Ma wanted to systematically track the frontiers of innovation in these two sectors globally and to be able to invest selectively where they identified opportunities.

Today, the Global Voyager Fund has deployed just under US$500 million of capital and is typically a growth stage investor in companies five to eight years old. While the fund focuses on companies that are getting close to breakeven with a solid revenue stream and customer base, they also look at how the technology the target has can be used in the Ping An ecosystem of companies or if some of Ping An's capabilities can be embedded within the target's business model to enhance it.

For example, the Global Voyager Fund has invested in Silicon Valley-based H2O.ai. The company uses the combination of open-source models and sophisticated editing tools to build AI models much faster. This "collapses the process of building an AI model from about 6-12 weeks to just three to seven days," Larsen explained.

Today, H2O.ai's platform is hosted on the Ping An cloud, allowing it to be offered to other financial institutions in China to help H2O.ai expand their business to Asia.

Another example is US-based Snapsheet, the largest new generation claims management platform provider in the US. The company supports seven of the top 10 auto insurers in the US market. As mentioned at the beginning of the chapter, Ping An is the largest auto insurer in the world and has developed a visual claims analysis module – a capability Snapsheet was missing and that is now integrated into their stack thanks to Ping An coming on board as an investor.

Ping An hosts their visual claims module on AWS in the US to make it accessible to Snapsheet's clients. By investing in Snapsheet and integrating Ping An's own capabilities, the group was able to find a direct channel to seven of the top 10 US car insurers. If Ping An had tried to enter the market with this technology themselves, it most likely would have been much more challenging and would have taken longer to get access to those companies.

This example shows that Ping An is much more than a retail financial services group and the reason why many refer to it as a tech company. In China, the group has established its ecosystem of internet companies that today support their insurance and financial services business. In addition, Ping An Group has ventured into the SaaS business globally and is importing and exporting technology innovation directly and through the venture investments it makes.

What is remarkable in their setup, regardless of which venture you look at, Ping An aims to dominate the space by leveraging their infrastructure, assets and knowledge across the group. Its large ecosystem in China allows the company to introduce promising new technologies from the West into the Chinese market, benefitting from rapid scaling by investing in those companies with this more integrated mindset between the target company and Ping An. It is the opposite of siloed thinking across businesses or geographies that many companies default to.

In order to scale globally, Ping An invests in promising and often well-established fintechs and insurtechs that give the company access to western markets. This way, they can monetize their inhouse development and market it globally.

I have not come across any other examples of financial services conglomerates that have mastered playing in such a wide range of verticals and combining them in a meaningful way.

Coming back to the three success factors mentioned at the beginning of this chapter, Ping An's success is driven by its:
1. Unique ecosystem approach,
2. Culture that embraces new technologies, and
3. The overall entrepreneurial spirit of the company.

Their culture and entrepreneurial mindset is what really makes Ping An unique and sets the company apart from other major insurance groups. The company is highly opportunistic, looks beyond the core insurance and financial services business and has an open mind for any type of innovation that can be turned into a profitable business model.

The fact that Ping An offers its cutting-edge technology to competitors is remarkable in an industry that historically has viewed inhouse technological innovations as a competitive advantage that should not be disclosed. However, Ping An, like Amazon with AWS, sees more opportunity in turning those capabilities into yet another business model than keeping them to itself.

This strategy not only allows Ping An to create new revenue streams but also helps its technology to advance as new use cases and more data will only improve the model.

Insurers across the globe are focused on change management and trying to develop a culture and mindset that embraces change and fosters innovation. Ping An has reinvented itself more than once in the past 35 years.

Ma, as the founder who is still involved in the company as group chairman, has a major impact on the overall mindset and culture at Ping An. He was able to preserve that entrepreneurial spirit in a company that today has over 350,000 employees. His vision and leadership enabled Ping An to become a global leader in financial services.

While no other company can replicate Ma or may not have living founders around today to keep involved in the business, the lessons from his leadership and how Ping An looks at new opportunities and investments can be replicated if you have the willingness to adopt such an approach.

Foundations for The Future

- Mindset and culture are the top success factors for innovation and need a strong leader to be developed.

- When launching a corporate venture, make sure it is setup as a startup and not another corporate project. For a venture to be successful it needs autonomy and accountability to investors.

- New ventures that can add to your existing business, or where your business can help the venture succeed are better fits strategically and financially for any corporate venture.

10. Tune Protect

Southeast Asia, also referred to as the ASEAN region, is composed of eleven countries each with its own unique history, culture and diversity of religions. What connects them all is low-cost airline carrier, AirAsia, with its famous tagline 'Now Everyone Can Fly' and the goal to democratize air travel.

AirAsia started in Malaysia in 2001 and quickly grew from two aircraft into the fourth largest airline in Asia with more than 200 planes. Over the last 20 years, AirAsia has evolved into an investment holding company known as Capital A with a portfolio of synergistic travel and lifestyle businesses. Their strategy is to offer the best value at the lowest cost.[49]

By stripping away services that most travelers do not need, AirAsia can offer comparatively cheap base ticket fares. When I was living in Bangkok, I often used the airline when I wanted to spend a weekend in Vietnam. I really didn't need a check-in bag for a two-day trip or a meal on the short, one-hour flight. On other occasions when having a long-haul flight, however, I had to check my luggage and wanted a bit more comfort. Like many low-cost carriers, AirAsia offers additional services like premium seats with more legroom or checked luggage at an additional cost.

This strategy of breaking down a product and offering the option to purchase each component individually is what we are witnessing in the insurance industry as well and what is often referred to as bite-sized or small-ticket insurance. One insurer that learned this strategy directly from AirAsia is Tune Protect (Tune).

In 2011, Tune was incorporated under the Tune Group which was established by the same founders of Capital A to serve the travel and hospitality business of AirAsia and the Tune Group. At the time,

---

[49] "About Us," AirAsia, as of 20 October 2022.

AirAsia was booming, and the travel insurance business was very profitable. As a result, the newly formed holding company could rely on AirAsia as its sole distribution channel.

Having a reliable sales channel was not the only advantage of being part of AirAsia. Despite being an airline, AirAsia had strong technology capabilities. After all, the airline was set up to distribute tickets digitally and had created their own digital membership program and a one-stop travel, e-commerce and fintech super app.

Their technology strength rubbed off on Tune. "The tech we had for AirAsia was quite advanced and, at some point, we realized why don't we just use this for the other businesses? Why should we restrict it to the AirAsia business? That's how we've grown out to the market more broadly," explained Rohit Nambiar, Tune Protect Group CEO.

Today, the Tune Protect Group consists of licensed insurers in Malaysia and Thailand, a digital distribution business in the Middle East, an insurtech that is focused on providing technology both internally and as an offering to external partners, and a licensed reinsurer in Malaysia specializing in bite-sized insurance cover that operates in over 45 countries.

Despite their rapid growth, Tune is still a very small player and had to find its niche in the market. Product-wise the insurer focuses on what already made AirAsia successful, breaking up a comprehensive product into smaller components, so consumers can buy exactly want they need without any frills or being turned off from buying by the cost of things they don't value.

According to Nambiar, there are two types of consumers. One category is wealthier and more mature insurance customers. This group is looking for comprehensive products with high level of convenience. Hence this group predominantly buys from an insurance agent or broker as they do not want to waste time conducting their own product research.

Nambiar described this as a red ocean market, that is, an existing market with fierce competition where insurers try to outperform their rivals on who gives a better feature. And sometimes the features are just a bit of a gimmick to try to score a point over the other players.

The second group Nambiar sees are Millennials and Generation Z. "For them, three things matter: price, simplicity of the process, and transparency," Nambiar explained. This customer segment is looking for the kind of bite-sized products Tune focuses on.

Millennials and Generation Z are an important and growing market for all insurers, especially in Southeast Asia. The median age in the region is 30.2 years, compared to 42.5 in Europe and 38.3 in the US.[50] Yet many insurers are still mainly focused on the older generation which is still considered the more profitable segment as insurers can sell comprehensive products at higher margins. However, sooner or later all insurers will have to focus on the next generation of customers, and this will mean adjustments to existing products to meet the wants and needs of a new generation of buyers.

It is naïve to think the younger generation will simply want the exact same products as their parents as they age and mature. As it has always been the case and increasingly so in a more digital world, lifestyle and therefore risks have changed significantly. Therefore, many insurers are struggling to resonate with Millennials and Generation Z and to understand their needs because existing products and approaches to the market are designed for the needs and expectations of older generations.

"If somebody is getting the Young Leader of the Year Award at 39, something is wrong with our industry."

– Rohit Nambiar Group CEO, Tune Protect Group

Insurers' struggle to appeal to younger generations applies not only to attracting younger customers but also to attracting talent to work in the industry. In the US, the median age of insurance industry employees is 45,[51] and we see a similar picture in Asia. Nambiar shared, "at 39, I won the Young Leader of the Year Award at the Asia Insurance Review Awards. I mentioned in my speech that if somebody is getting the Young Leader of the Year Award at 39, something is wrong with our industry."

The reality is that the insurance industry is often not a very attractive employer for younger people. Nambiar shared that in his previous company as well as within Tune, the employee NPS scores are very good for older segments but are dropping significantly for lower age groups of employees. He said, "For the age groups 45-plus and 50-

---

[50] "World Population," World-o-meter, as of 22 April 2023.
[51] Hilton, John, "Insurers Working Quickly To Address Employee Shortage Crisis" Insurance Newsweek, 5 May 2022.

plus, scores tend to be very good. The minute it's age 30, it's bad. 25 is terrible."

Lack of young talent may in fact be one of the reasons insurers are struggling to design products for Millennials and Generation Z. Product development within insurance companies is often predominantly driven internally by the Actuarial or Underwriting teams and not so much by market research or customer insights. With a median age of 45, it comes as no surprise that many products have been designed with the older generation in mind and are focused on the risks and fears they face.

Therefore, diversity of age groups, genders, cultures and socioeconomic backgrounds is highly important to develop new and innovative products so that different perspectives and needs can be more deeply understood and accounted for by those developing and designing insurance products.

Another often-cited challenge to developing innovative products is the constraints of legacy systems. Outdated backend and frontend systems do not allow insurers to quickly react to new market opportunities and launch new products to market quickly or with the kind of customer experience increasingly digital consumers expect – especially younger consumers.

> "Tech is over glorified in our industry... Tech is very important. Yes, that's why we're able to move fast. But first is culture. Build the right culture, get the right people, and then comes tech."
>
> – Rohit Nambiar
> Group CEO,
> Tune Protect Group

Tune is still a relatively new player with less of a legacy issue and, thanks to its association with AirAsia, the insurer has a strong emphasis on technology. This is what gives the young insurer an edge over their competition. "I can't compete with the AIAs and Prudentials and AXAs of the world on anything else, but what I can compete on is my speed," explained Nambiar. He continued, "if you find someone faster than Tune, show it to me. I bet you can't. And I mean it. I don't think anybody in Southeast Asia can execute faster than us. And I'm ready for this challenge. That's our most powerful differentiator today."

However, according to Nambiar, the company's speed is not only enabled by technology. Three components play a role – culture, people and tech – with tech deliberately listed last. Nambiar explained, "Tech is over glorified in our industry. Everybody says, 'Put millions of dollars on tech and suddenly everything will be sorted.' Tech is very important. Yes, that's why we're able to move fast. But first is culture. Build the right culture, get the right people, and then comes tech."

In many ways, technology is the easiest of the three. Even if companies do not have the internal skills to build cutting edge technology, there are many great suppliers in the market, from well-established software providers to new SaaS insurtechs, that can help insurers build their tech.

Culture and people, on the other hand, must be developed internally in an often complex and lengthy journey. Many organizations have identified culture as a crucial component but very few have really cracked the code on how to build an enduring one that embraces change and innovation.

For Nambiar, culture starts from the top. In his view, the management team must demonstrate leadership in innovation and accept the risks and uncertainty that come with it.

The concept of 'fail fast and fail often' has been very popular in the startup and tech worlds. This does not mean failure is encouraged but it is an accepted risk when being innovative. It also means you must be willing to learn from mistakes quickly and tweak your next attempt accordingly.

In the insurance industry, and specifically if we look at major product launches that have been months or even years in the making, failure is not naturally something many embrace. You could argue that Tune, with its bite-sized products that are launched in an agile manner, has more room for failure. However, Nambiar dismisses the idea that size or complexity can be an excuse for not embracing failure. He shared that he followed the same attitude towards failure at his previous company, which is one of the largest insurance groups globally. He said, "if you're not ready to be fired, you're never going to innovate."

At Tune, Nambiar shares with his team his stories of failure to encourage this mindset and to lead from the top. He explained "I became a CEO at 37, and I have failed so many times. Failing for known, avoidable reasons; sabotage; fraud – that's a different point. There's no tolerance for that. But failing for honest reasons is part of the culture. It's something that I always speak to the teams about, so they understand the idea."

Another strategy Nambiar applies within Tune is a concept he simply calls, "Yes". Every two months, he runs a strategy meeting with 30 employees. The employees come from across different parts of the organization to discuss new ideas. While those ideas are discussed, nobody can say anything negative about it.

> "As insurers, for too long we have been looking at what will not work rather than what will work."
>
> – Rohit Nambiar
> Group CEO,
> Tune Protect Group

"Why do we do this? As insurers, for too long we have been looking at what will not work rather than what will work," Nambiar explained. Therefore, those meetings are designed to let ideas flow freely. People can agree, can add value to an idea, but at this stage, they are not allowed to criticize it in any way.

At the end of the meeting, the team will have come up with 20-30 ideas and all members will vote for the top three ideas. The basis for the vote is which idea you would invest your own money into.

Once the top three ideas have been chosen, the next stage starts where risks and challenges are analyzed. Here, some ideas will fall off as they are not feasible or deemed too risky. The ideas that make it through this stage, however, have the buy in from the entire team, which is almost as important as the idea itself.

Especially when it comes to innovative ideas that have never been done before, a commitment from the teams involved is crucial. Navigating the complex landscape of insurance regulation and the technical requirements needed to make something new happen is no easy task. I have seen many projects fail because the teams involved were not motivated to deal with the complexity and find a solution. They lacked the commitment and personal buy-in needed to be willing to work through the complexity and effort required for success.

Nambiar's "Yes" concept is a clever strategy to get the commitment of the various teams across the company. Afterall, a majority of the 30 team members would have voted for the idea and got excited by it, which means the risk of them turning around after a few weeks and saying the idea is not feasible or worth pursuing is much lower. To them, it became their idea in many respects, so they want to make it work. This is what gives them the motivation to work through the difficult moments, as will the knowledge that there is acceptance of failure should things ultimately not work out.

A culture that accepts the risk of failure also leads to a culture that feels comfortable making decisions. This is a crucial component if your biggest differentiator in the market is your speed since you can't be fast if you get stuck in the face of tough (or simple) decisions. "Make a decision, even if it's wrong. The worst thing to do is to not make a decision," Nambiar explained.

To increase the speed of decision-making, Nambiar has adopted a very informal communication strategy. He says, "I don't use email. I use WhatsApp. My team knows emails are dead for me. So, if they have something more involved and do need to send an email, they will also send me a WhatsApp message to be sure I know to check my emails."

Communicating more directly certainly drives speed in decision making. However, it can also increase the risk of miscommunication due to a lack of detail or context. Applying this kind of communication and decision-making strategy certainly is only possible in a culture that is accepting of failure and values speed to market more than identifying who is responsible for making a mistake.

Nambiar was able to reduce the time to market for what usually takes the industry on average 8-10 months to launch, to just three months – or even less. In June 2020, at the height of the global COVID-19 pandemic, Tune was able to launch a health insurance cover for travel within a newly defined travel bubble within only three days. This allowed them to seize on a new and likely time-limited opportunity in the market. It took other insurers several months to launch a product and Nambiar recalled "We really grabbed the market opportunity and owned the space."

Of course, not all product launches are successes. Nambiar admitted that in general, due to the short time to launch, the team likely makes more mistakes than they would with a longer planning period. However, the detriment of the mistakes is not generally significant and the value of their speed to market is greater than any such costs.

This is especially true when the team can't be sure how consumers will respond to a product until it is launched. Nambiar shared, "We have launched products where we've only sold four policies at launch. And there have been policies where we've sold to 130,000 customers and generated MYR 12 million (~ US$2.6 million) in premium in the first month alone."

Before launching a product, Tune conducts ethnographic research and focus groups. Similar to the experience of OneDegree, they discovered that regardless of how much research they conduct, they will only know if it works when they launch a product.

"If you ask me which product will succeed and which one will fail at launch, I will tell you I actually have no clue! Sometimes my ethnographic research comes back saying this product is going to be a killer. Then, after launch, however, we realize this product doesn't work." Nambiar shared.

The high risk of failure of a product launch is amplified by Tune's business model of selling direct to consumers. A traditional insurer with an agency force often has high confidence that a well-engineered product can be sold by well-incentivized agents. With digital distribution, the consumer is making the choice and, therefore, only products that appeal to the consumer can be sold successfully.

Nambiar believes that consumers know exactly what they want and, in many cases, do not need a salesperson to make a decision for them. He shared, "We let the customer choose. Some people believe customers do not know what they want. I think that's exactly the problem we created for ourselves by saying we know what the consumer wants, without even telling the consumer what they're buying."

> "Making things simple is very complex. That's why we as an industry make things complex – because it's very simple."
>
> – Rohit Nambiar
> Group CEO,
> Tune Protect Group

Selling direct to consumers requires that products are easily understandable and transparent. However, many products in insurance are highly complex with long terms and conditions and a range of exclusions. Nambiar said, "Making things simple is very complex. That's why we as an industry make things complex – because it's very simple."

Tune has broken down a range of products into smaller, easy to understand components. For example, the insurer offer 14 different travel insurance components including baggage protection, different health covers and flight delay, to name just a few. Customers can pick and choose what is most important to their individual situation and works within their budget.

Tune applies the same strategy to its critical illness coverage. The customer can decide which critical illnesses he or she wants to include in their policy, without having to pay for others they don't see value in protecting against or don't want to spend on buying cover for.

Having simple products is not only important so customers can understand the value proposition but also to providing a seamless customer experience.

For Tune, Nambiar has adopted a philosophy that is called "ThreeThreeThree." What is behind this philosophy is a promise to their customers that:

- Within three minutes, they can buy a policy,
- Within three hours, they will hear back regarding an enquiry, and
- Within three days, Tune will pay out their claim upon approval.

Today, Tune is paying out 87% of claims within three days. Within nine months, Tune was able to turn its initially-negative NPS positive, from -16% to +14%,[52] and to +39% in December 2022.[53] This was achieved by truly understanding what matters most to their customers and delivering on that front consistently.

Apart from the B2C side, Tune has ventured into the B2B2C space in over 45 countries. They work with over 75 partners, including telecommunication companies, airlines, ride hailing and taxi platforms, ecommerce platforms, travel sites and health companies.

Initially Tune's strategy was to redirect customers from a partner's website to their own. However, in Nambiar's experience, this approach does not work very well.

With his previous company, he had worked on a partnership project with a telecommunication company. While the insurer got a lot of traffic from the telecommunication company, they had a very low conversion rate. Nambiar shared that, "for every 1000 customers sent over, only five bought a policy."

Rearranging the landing page in an effort to improve the customer journey only led to a small increase in sales. What changed the game, however, was moving the sales process entirely to the website of the telecommunication provider as an embedded offering.

"The consumer wants to associate with the telecommunication brand and not with us as the insurer in this case," explained Nambiar. He added "When you're buying a legacy planning product, brand definitely matters. When you're buying a comprehensive health

---

[52] "Annual Report 2021," Tune Protect, 16 October 2022.
[53] "Annual Report 2022," Tune Protect, 28 July 2023.

product, the brand matters. But when you're buying bite-sized travel insurance or you are buying motor insurance, which is a highly commoditized product, the brand doesn't matter as much because you're buying it from someone who you trust, and you have the belief that they have an insurance partner who will deliver. Your trust is more with the original brand you associated yourself with and not the insurance provider partnering with that brand."

Today, Tune offers what Nambiar calls 'insurance in a box' in four lines of business: lifestyle insurance such as travel; home or gadget insurance; simple health coverage; and SME products specifically for the gig economy. The majority of their partners distribute their business online but Tune also works with a few offline partners.

This insurance in the box concept allows partners to integrate an insurance offering into their business model in a relatively straightforward manner. The offering is developed by Tune's in-house insurtech business called White Label and includes integration via APIs that cover the entire value chain from quote, to buying a product, to admin and all the way to e-claims. In addition, White Label offers dashboards for reporting and data analytics capabilities.

Because Tune only has an insurance license in Malaysia and Thailand, they partner with over 30 local underwriters in other markets. Those local insurers often have a larger balance sheet than Tune, but do not have the capabilities to offer bite-sized insurance products direct to consumers, making it attractive to them to partner with Tune. Nambiar shared, "We have a couple of partners who are at least four or five times bigger than us. They tell us that, in lifestyle insurance, we lead the conversation because we understand digital very well."

A lack of the technology needed is often one reason those local insurers cannot compete selling digitally direct to consumers. The other reason is product creation. As mentioned earlier, designing a product that is easy to understand and transparent is crucial to success, but also very difficult to do. Because of this complexity, the technical investment needed together with relatively lower average premium when compared to traditional insurance products, some insurers don't believe that bite-sized products can be profitable.

Nambiar shared, "I do know some insurers were uncomfortable working with us because they think we are cowboys. We aren't – our loss ratios are the proof. We are a listed company so anybody can look at our loss ratio. It is lower than the industry average everywhere we work." In 2021, Tune's net claims incurred ratio was 19.3%, while the industry's was 49.9%.[54]

What also helps Tune to convince insurance partners is their reinsurance capability. Tune's Malaysian reinsurer allows them to offer the reinsurance needed for their bite-sized products and demonstrates to partners that they have some skin in the game, as well.

The way Tune chooses a partner comes down to culture and mindset, again. Nambiar shared that they look for partners that are willing to work on an offering together and put the customer first. In the insurance industry and especially if we look at bancassurance partnerships, it is very common for an insurer to pay a large upfront fee to the partner to secure the business relationship. Therefore, the selection of a partner is often not based on what is best for the customer, but a pure short-term revenue decision of who pays the most.

Nambiar explained "the minute you go down that route of upfront payments, one party is on top and it's never an equal conversation. The minute you go here, you become a sales junkie. It's a terrible relationship and you're never aligned."

Through its own direct to consumer business and its partnerships, Tune has access to over 150 million customers. The company has managed to find its niche in a market that is often overlooked and considered by many not to be profitable. "We will not be number one in any market. We might be number one in a couple of segments, but not in the market overall," explained Nambiar. His focus is on being a disruptor in the bite-sized insurance market and a leader when it comes to NPS.

NPS is one KPI that is very important for Tune. In addition, Nambiar uses a lot of leading KPIs like search engine rankings, traffic on the website, bounce rate, and number of customers. "Eventually this will create enterprise value and top- and bottom-line results. I don't just measure these things for initiatives or just to watch metrics," explained Nambiar.

What defines a successful bite-sized insurance business is the ability to bind a large number of small policies on a regular basis to develop

---

[54] "Annual Report 2021," Tune Protect, 16 October 2022.

a stable and profitable portfolio. Many small steps and decisions are needed to get to this point, and failure will be part of the journey.

As Nambiar has explained, some products will fail, and many in the team might be disappointed by that. Especially if it was a jointly developed idea with broad buy-in from those involved.

Therefore, another component that is important in Tune's corporate culture is celebrating small successes. Nambiar explained, "I need to celebrate success, so people constantly see the positive actions Tune is taking."

Celebrating successes, especially the small ones, is something that is often missing in large organizations. In 2021, I joined a project where the entire team was working under a lot of pressure over several months, but never celebrated any successes. The team became disenchanted with the project, leading most of them to be satisfied with mediocre efforts and outcomes. They just wanted to be done and were not motivated to go the extra mile or crack a difficult problem.

I noticed myself how this culture and mindset affected me and drained my energy. You can have the best people and the latest technology, but if your culture doesn't embrace change; if you cannot motivate and inspire people; you will find it very difficult to innovate and succeed.

This lesson is clearly engrained at Tune Protect, and how they have been able to succeed as they have.

Foundations for The Future

- Technology is important but people and culture are more important.

- A culture that embraces innovation must be motivated to tackle the difficult questions, be accepting of failure and feel comfortable to make decisions.

- Playing in a specific niche often comes with playing by different rules. Every organization has to set their definition of what success looks like and what are the tools to get there.

- The path to success comes with wins and losses that each need to be recognized, learned from, accepted and celebrated.

11. Habitto

I think of the future of insurance as a mosaic made up of innovative ideas. Some pieces are fresh and not yet tested. Others have already been proven to work well.

This poses an intriguing question: once an idea has been tested and validated, does it still represent the future? Does the true nature of the future rely on new ideas that are still unproven and have yet to show success?

As I embarked on the journey of writing this book, a key debate emerged: should I profile an early-stage startup which is defined by its unproven yet potentially groundbreaking ideas, or should I focus on proven players whose innovative concepts have been tested, refined, and have ultimately borne fruit?

On the one hand, featuring an early-stage startup offers a glimpse into the uncertain yet tantalizing future. Such ventures, driven by raw ambition and novel ideas, embody the spirit of exploration and risk-taking that often fuels transformative change. Yet, their stories are inextricably linked with uncertainty.

On the other hand, focusing on proven players brings a degree of certainty and a grounding in the reality of what has been achieved. Their innovations, once novel ideas, have successfully navigated implementation and market acceptance, morphing from potential game-changers to actual change agents. Yet, one might question, once the novelty wears off and an idea becomes the norm, does it still represent the future, or has it simply become part of the present?

As I delved deeper into this conundrum, I found myself engaged in a profound conversation with Samantha Ghiotti, the CEO and co-founder of Habitto. As she shared her journey, I realized that hers was a narrative I needed to weave into this book.

Ghiotti's story isn't merely the chronicle of a new venture; it's an embodiment of the cycle of innovation itself. It's about a team harnessing lessons from previous entrepreneurial experiences across different sectors, dedicating themselves to deeply understanding customer needs and the psychology of purchasing behaviors. This is a story about demonstrating the audacity to grapple with the challenging questions the industry hasn't solved, about embracing the uncertainty of the unproven, and daring to take a shot against seemingly insurmountable odds.

In featuring Ghiotti's journey with Habitto, we find a compelling fusion of the known and the unknown, the proven and the unproven. Here, the essence of the future of insurance comes to life: a combination of tested insights applied to uncharted possibilities, a balancing act that brings vibrancy and excitement to the evolving narrative of insurance innovation.

In addition, it gives me the opportunity to shine some light on a very different Asian market, Japan.

As explained in the opening chapters of this book, it's an oversimplification to generalize Asia. Every country within this vast continent is rich in unique culture and history, and therefore faces distinct challenges.

Japan's demographic profile distinctly sets it apart from other Asian countries discussed in this book, serving as a microcosm that mirrors many of the characteristics of Western Europe and a substantial part of North America. Its population is marked by a high level of education and an advanced median age; a stark contrast to the youthful populations in many emerging Asian markets.

The median age in Indonesia stands at 31.1, and, in India, it is 28.7. In contrast, the United States has a median age of 38.5 while Singapore's median age is 35.6. Yet, Japan stands apart. It shows the highest median age globally at 48.6. Its closest counterparts are Germany with a median age of 47.8, Italy at 46.5, and Hong Kong at 45.6.[55]

By spotlighting Japan and the story of Habitto, I plan to present a different facet of the insurance innovation narrative. One that not only captures the spirit of an early-stage startup but also illustrates the impact of unique demographic, cultural, and historical contexts on the course of innovation and maybe the ultimate future the insurance industry is facing.

---

[55] "Median age by country," World Data, 23 May 2023.

The unique demographic reality of Japan serves as a crystal ball into what could be the future for many mature countries that are facing the issue of an aging population coupled with long life expectancy. The combination of these two dynamics in Japan introduces specific challenges and opportunities that have substantial implications for the insurance industry, and, by extension, broader sphere of financial services.

An aging population presents a variety of challenges, including a rise in healthcare demands and costs due to an increased prevalence of chronic illnesses and age-related diseases. Longer life expectancy places a strain on social security and pension systems due to a larger population relying on these forms of retirement income for longer and a smaller proportion paying into them. The workforce may shrink, leading to labor shortages and a higher dependency ratio, causing potential economic slowdown. The fiscal pressure on public spending to meet these demands can lead to significant political and economic challenges.

As countries like the United States and Germany trend towards a similar demographic shift, the innovative strategies and solutions employed by Japanese startups and established companies alike could provide valuable insights and models for other nations. In particular, Japan's experience can offer critical lessons on how to adapt insurance products and services to cater to an aging society without losing sight of the next generation and their needs.

By examining Habitto's journey to enter the Japanese market, the challenges they have identified and the potential they see could help us understand how the evolving demographic makeup of societies worldwide may shape the future of insurance. The recent story of Japan helps us see that there is not only potential in growth markets, but also in reshaping mature markets. However, it might need someone with a new perspective to identify what needs to change, which represents a huge opportunity for insurtech startups. Unfortunately, Japan's insurtech scene isn't as vibrant as some of its neighbors.

While we see Japanese companies investing in insurtech globally, like Tokio Marine's investment in bolttech, there are only a few insurtechs that have started in Japan and even fewer that have gained exposure globally. "Japan, with a population of 120 million people, has less than two dozen home-grown insurtechs, and most of them are

B2B," explained Ghiotti. In October 2022, Sønr published a list of the world's top 100 insurtechs. While 18 insurtechs on the list are from Asia, not one of them is from Japan.[56]

This is a surprising reality given that Japan is the third largest insurance market worldwide in terms of premium. The sheer size of the Japanese insurance market can largely be attributed to the awareness the Japanese population holds about the value of insurance, with an impressive 90% of households maintaining life insurance coverage.[57] "In Japan, people think about insurance as a byproduct of the social construct of looking after each other. There's a deeply rooted social contract to look after your loved ones and to support them in times of need," explained Ghiotti.

However, the unique demographics heavily impact the insurance industry and how it has developed in terms of products and distribution. According to an article published by The Actuary Magazine, over 50% of assets are held by individuals 65 and older.[58] This concentration of wealth prompted many insurance companies to primarily target this older demographic in their distribution strategies, with agency distribution accounting for over 90% of general insurance sales in 2021.[59]

Ghiotti shared, "Whenever I speak to Japanese insurers today, they bemoan the fact that their customer base is dying and they are struggling to appeal to the newer generation. The traditional face-to-face, tied agency model could not be further away from how the young generation expects to be talked to, engaged and serviced."

With Habitto, she now aims to address this issue and leverage the lessons she has learned throughout her career. Ghiotti has worked for over twenty years at the intersection of technology and financial services across four continents. In 2019, she moved to Singapore as the deputy CEO of Singlife. At the time, Singlife was struggling to grow as a web-based insurer and Ghiotti helped to pivot the company to a mobile-first financial services company.

---

[56] "Insurtech 100," Sønr, 5 June 2022.
[57] Ma, Masu, "Changes, Opportunities and Challenges in the Japanese Insurance Market," *The Actuary Magazine*, 3 June 2023.
[58] *The Actuary Magazine*, 3 June 2023.
[59] "Direct Premiums by Type of Distribution Channels (Fiscal 2021)," The General Insurance Association of Japan, 31 July 2023.

"What we did really well at Singlife was to build a product that customers needed and actually wanted. Building products that people really want may seem obvious but surprisingly it is more of a happy accident in insurance, instead of a deliberate intention" she shared.

> "Building products that people really want may seem obvious but surprisingly it is more of a happy accident in insurance, instead of a deliberate intention."
>
> – Samantha Ghiotti
> Co-founder, Habitto

Upon the merger of Singlife and Aviva, Ghiotti and several of her colleagues chose to exit the company. Fueled by a passion to continue a journey of innovation, building things that people need, and contribute to the future trajectory of the industry led them to regroup. Their strategy relied on Ghiotti tapping into her fintech investing experience and the team drawing upon the insights garnered at Singlife and point that at a much larger market.

Ghiotti recalled, "We were specifically attracted by larger markets that had similar saving behaviors to Singapore and high insurance awareness. Japan was an obvious winner, though not without significant entry challenges."

It takes a group of people that are highly motivated, resourceful and creative, to tackle the challenges of starting a new business in Japan as a foreigner. It is a country that is known to be very insulated and tough to enter as an outsider which might be one of the reasons why Japan has not seen as many significant insurtech developments as markets like Singapore.

To be successful in such an environment, Ghiotti pointed out the importance of diversity, and not only in terms of gender, ethnicity and age. She explained, "It's also about the cognitive difference that is required to be able to come up with novel solutions for problems that are really hard to tackle. And I think there are many problems in the insurance industry that can benefit from an outsider perspective. So bringing to the table people that have a different approach to problem solving and sense making, can be very powerful."

Certainly, the Habitto founding team has a wide range of different backgrounds. Italian-born Ghiotti has worked as an operator for financial institutions as well as a venture investor; co-founder Liam McCance is an Australian entrepreneur with experience in brand and marketing across several sectors; Chief Product Officer André Bose do Amaral is Brazilian and has a strong background in product and user experience (UX) design.

Being true to the diversity agenda, Ghiotti has further grown the team and has added different backgrounds and complementary skillsets employing people from age 19 to 70, from sectors such as gaming, AI, entertainment, consumer tech, capital markets and insurance. As an insurtech business, Habitto has hired less than 15% of staff from within the insurance industry.

With this diverse team, Ghiotti is now planning to enter the market and cater to the younger generation following a mobile-first strategy. "We're addressing a difficult and important societal problem, that of the young generation being left behind by large financial institutions. The young population has different needs and preferences when it comes to buying products, and I think all financial institutions really struggle to make sense of that and to become relevant for this new customer segment. Japan as an overall market has always struggled with growth over the last 20-odd years. So the two biggest strategic questions for any financial institution in Japan are: How do you become relevant to the younger population? And how do you grow?" Ghiotti explained.

The team at Habitto conducted extensive primary and secondary research on customer behavior and needs before making the decision to enter the Japanese market. This kind of research is a practice I've noticed many startups excel at, compared to established businesses. After all, the success of startups frequently hinges on the introduction of a product that genuinely satisfies consumer needs and offers a seamless user journey. While existing insurance companies can somewhat depend on their pre-existing sales networks to introduce a product to the market, newcomers need to create a product that naturally draws in customers.

Since the team came together in 2021, Habitto has obsessed over better understanding customer needs. They found that the young generation is increasingly worried about future aspects of their lives, such as their life span, how long they will have to work, healthcare affordability, and their ability to provide for their children's education and their octogenarian parents. These concerns are universal across different cultures but are significantly heightened in Japan due to the exceptionally long average lifespans, particularly among women who are likely to outlive their partners by several years. The team even consulted with psychologists and discovered that people seek psychological support for financial issues more frequently in Japan than in any other market they have studied.

"We were surprised by the level of financial anxiety in Japan, especially in women and in people in their thirties and forties. Many have not taken any action towards building their financial wellness, stashing away their hard earned cash in zero-yielding bank accounts. They know they have a shorter runway, don't know what to do, who to trust. No wonder, they stress about it." Ghiotti shared.

> "We were surprised by the level of financial anxiety in Japan, especially in women and in people in their thirties and forties ."
>
> – Samantha Ghiotti
> Co-founder, Habitto

The team also unpacked some interesting insights around the relevance of many financial experiences for women. Ghiotti shared, that, "if you speak to women, they often mention feeling neglected or belittled by financial institutions. We heard women saying, 'if I meet an insurance agent or a broker with my husband, I get a certain treatment, but if I go by myself, I feel I get a different treatment'."

Japan, despite being one of the most advanced countries in the world, has a large gender equity gap. In the 2022 Gender Gap Report by the World Economic Forum, Japan ranks last (#19) for the East Asia and Pacific region while Singapore is at #4 and Indonesia is at #10. The report also shows that gender equality in economic participation and opportunity has further declined in recent years. The share of women in legislative, senior and managerial positions decreased by 9.8% while men's share increased by +2.6%.[60]

Habitto aims to make financial services more relatable, by combining tech and human empathy through a mobile-first strategy, targeting not only the youth but placing a significant emphasis on women. There certainly is a need and an opportunity for this focus with women constituting over half of Japan's population. The trend of unmarried women is on an upswing, particularly among those with a

---

[60] "Global Gender Gap Report 2022," World Economic Forum, 3 June 2023.

higher education, who seem to show a predilection towards remaining single.[61]

After thorough research, Ghiotti and her team concluded that a holistic strategy was necessary to equip the young generation with the tools to attain financial freedom. This meant not just providing advice on insurance, but also integrating elements of banking and wealth management. The overarching aim was to empower the youth to navigate their financial futures with confidence and with the support of genuine financial advice.

However, the right product strategy won't take you far if the regulatory environment won't allow you to execute your idea. Ghiotti believes, "a lot of financial innovation comes from regulatory opening." I think there's more to it. Evidently, without regulatory adjustments, even straightforward innovations such as electronic signatures are unachievable. However, I believe that without progressive companies advocating for these changes, regulatory modifications would either not transpire or occur at a lethargic pace.

In the case of Habitto, however, it was a change in regulation that opened the door. A significant regulatory change that harmonized the distribution of financial products enabled the launch of a connected financial experience in Japan. The new regulation allows the distribution of banking, securities and insurance products under one license and one harmonized framework.

In the past, companies needed a different distribution license for each vertical, which is cost-prohibitive for an early-stage startup. With the New Financial Services Intermediary Legislation that came into effect in November 2021, financial services intermediaries are now able to offer products and services across multiple verticals, such as banking, securities, and insurance, under this new registration system. Habitto was the fifth financial services intermediary to register this license and the first foreign company to do so.

Navigating local regulations and partners as well as interpreting customer insights would not have been possible without the help of local experts as the founding team had no direct ties or cultural references to Japan.

---

[61] Raymo, J.M., "The second demographic transition in Japan: a review of the evidence," China popul. dev. stud. 6, 267–287, 2022.

"Building a human middleware was mission critical for us and an intentional organizational design principle. We needed to equip ourselves with the ability of absorbing and translating market insights, signals and norms into business practices we can understand and implement. From an organization design perspective, this is not simply a language translation layer but a deep meaning making and normalization capability, to enable a culturally diverse team like us operate effectively in Japan." Shared Ghiotti.

Habitto made two significant appointments early on: Kashiwagi-san, formerly CFO of Nomura Holdings, as advisor, and Kume-san, former CEO of BNP Cardiff, as COO.

It isn't always easy to get seasoned industry experts to join an early-stage startup. Partly because startups cannot afford corporate level compensation and partly because the risk of failure is too high for most executives to jump ship from a stable job to a startup. Equally, even when seasoned executives make the leap, their ability to be effective in a startup environment can often be questionable and this increases the startup's risk profile. In other words, hiring seasoned executives early on is a double-edged sword.

> *"From an organization design perspective, this is not simply a language translation layer but a deep meaning making and normalization capability, to enable a culturally diverse team like us operate effectively in Japan."*
>
> *– Samantha Ghiotti*
> *Co-founder, Habitto*

Ghiotti shared that, "With hindsight, getting Kume-san and Kashiwagi-san onboard was an act of serendipity. We worked very hard at building and nurturing our network to help us enter the Japan market and Kume-san and Kashiwagi-san are the lucky byproduct of that networking strategy."

Kume-san had just left his previous role at BNP Cardiff after 10 years as CEO and was, "looking to jump into something fresh, consumer focused and with a social purpose. Habitto was a perfect fit." Explained Ghiotti.

Kashiwagi-san was attracted by "the outside in perspective and radically novel approach to solve an entrenched social problem".

The successful recruitment of two seasoned industry experts by Habitto, thanks to their extensive professional networks, underscores the high regard the team commands within Asia's insurance industry. It also signifies the faith these experts have in Habitto's vision.

After assembling the team, getting the New Financial Services Intermediary License was the first major challenge for Habitto. The startup had raised US$3.4 million in Seed Funding but couldn't get started without a license. This posed a significant operational risk which was top of mind for the team and the investors.

Habitto managed to secure the requisite license in less than a year. Kume-san and Kashiwagi-san were instrumental in getting the license as they led and orchestrated that process. Ghiotti shared, "Without them, we, as two gaijin (foreigners in Japanese) founders, would likely still be navigating the process."

When Kume-san and Kashiwagi-san approached the Japanese regulator, they somewhat unexpectedly displayed large interest in Habitto's business model. It appears that the model perfectly aligned with what they envisioned when creating this new intermediary license and were thrilled to welcome foreign entrepreneurs.

The next challenge involved convincing partners to collaborate and provide products to distribute. As a mobile-first intermediary, Habitto needed partners to not only provide the products, but to integrate with their digital platform.

Kume-san proved crucial again, leading the efforts to establish these key relationships. Habitto began by partnering with Saison Asset Management, one of the three prospective partners they had identified in Japan, that held the Type 2 Asset Management license Habitto needed to be able to partner with them, and were already using it for direct-to-consumer distribution. The team at Habitto was determined to work directly with asset managers instead of having to access them through so-called Type 1 brokers to shorten the value chain. It was an added advantage that Saison Group was also an investor in Habitto, which bolstered a commercial decision that they were already committed to.

For their banking partner, Habitto launched an RFP process to assess the state of the Banking as a Service (BaaS) infrastructure in Japan. GMO Aozora Net Bank (GMOA) emerged as the frontrunner in this race due to their superior API library, although the market is very dynamic and contenders are quickly catching up.

With GMOA, Habitto designed what is their pull product, a simple savings account that offers a market leading interest rate. This is only possible because Habitto capped the maximum savings amount to one million Japanese Yen (~US$7,150) and is financing the interest with its customer acquisition costs (CAC). This is a strategy that is only sustainable if the team is able to cross-sell additional financial products with high margins to their clients, including insurance. Ghiotti shared, "this is an entry strategy that will require further adjustments to make it sustainable at scale."

Some might categorize Habitto as a fintech and not an insurtech but Ghiotti disagrees. She shared "our monetisation path is insurance via a bancassurance model. That makes us right on the bullseye of digital insurance, however, our initial go to market requires a pull proposition. That's why we focus on savings, which currently is delivered via a banking stack."

Bancassurance has seen considerable success across numerous Asian nations, yet the rise of mobile banking and the subsequent closure of physical bank branches are posing challenges. Despite the integration of insurance into online banking platforms, the conversion rates often fail to match those attained through face-to-face sales in brick-and-mortar branches or with the traditional agency distribution model.

The problem is that technology has its boundaries and many consumers, regardless of their financial literacy, want to talk to a human when it comes to decisions about their financial wellness that require taking risk (like investments) or buying products with multiple configurations (like most medical policies) or have long maturity (like term or whole life policies).

> *"Understanding the psychology of money decisions is really important, whether you're selling insurance, payments or financial assets."*
>
> *– Samantha Ghiotti*
> *Co-founder, Habitto*

Ghiotti and her team are planning to solve this issue and are working on the next generation of a digital bancassurance model. She explained, "What we're developing in Japan is a hybrid model that combines the power of technology with the power of people. It's basically the intersection of modern financial product distribution, coupled with the empathy building that only people can deliver. When it comes to making financial choices that involve taking risks, or multiple product configurations, having people talking to people helps tremendously in that decision making process. When choices become more complex, there are very few people, especially in Japan, that are willing to take that leap aided only by an algorithm. Understanding the psychology of money decisions is really important, whether you're selling insurance, payments or financial assets. So that's where we spent a lot of time and that's why Habitto is aiming to leverage technology and mobile distribution to deliver a very empathetic human experience."

In the model Habitto has developed, consumers have to download an app to gain access to their savings account, the pull-product that offers a best-in-market savings account. Once consumers are within the app, they are offered the chance to interact with a dedicated personal financial advisor. Interactions within the app are designed to be short, simple, and informal, while accommodating a variety of financial queries, no matter how trivial or complex. Furthermore, users can schedule video sessions with their advisors directly in the app. This is meant to accommodate the busy lives of customers, and a standard session only lasts around 10 minutes.

Advisors are trained to provide tailored advice across banking, investments, and insurance, considering each user's unique profile. If users decide to purchase any subsequent product through Habitto and its financial advisors, these products get incorporated into the app, allowing users to have a comprehensive view of their financial holdings.

What I find a very powerful feature of Habitto's app is the survey functionality. After each interaction with an advisor, users can rate their experience in terms of the advisory service received as well as the user experience. This helps Habitto get instant feedback for their financial advisors as well as on the user-friendliness of their app. In addition, Habitto can push surveys to users to discover more about their wants, needs and fears.

Ghiotti explained, "the mobile environment is perfect for personalization, data gathering and contextual experiences. Our advisors have a finger on their customers' pulse, in real time. Customers and advisors can share and access documentation as they share the same library of information."

Building a hybrid experience involves using technology to effectively scale human capacity. In Habitto's early journey, this aspect is particularly critical in order to develop a scalable operating model and viable business. The team has a clear understanding that the operating leverage of their business model rests heavily on their ability to scale the advisor layer. To this end, they've integrated AI and workflow automation tools, such as ChatGPT, to maximize the client-facing time of advisors by undertaking tasks like summarizing sessions, producing reports, and generating relevant content. Looking ahead, Habitto plans to further enhance its technology usage by constructing a product recommendation engine, implementing a next-best-action model, and automating much of the asynchronous communication between customers and advisors. Yet, they remain cautious about striking a balance between efficiency, achieved through these automations, and maintaining the relatability of the customer experience.

To begin the development journey, the startup was able to raise US$3.9 million in a Pre-series A round in October 2022, which brought the total funds raised to US$7.3 million. The next challenge for Habitto is acquiring customers. Often when starting out, the focus primarily lies on bringing customers through the door, disregarding metrics like unit economics and profitability. However, current market conditions and investor preferences emphasize early traction and revenue generation. This is especially true for Habitto, considering it is financing its high, market leading interest rates through its CAC. This makes the challenge and pressure to perform even more significant for the startup.

Habitto officially commenced operations in June 2023, making it premature to gauge its success at the time of this book's publication. As underscored in the OneDegree story, a staggering 90% of startups don't make it. Nonetheless, I am convinced that Habitto's team possesses the necessary skills to steer this startup towards success. Indeed, there may be a need to pivot or make some course corrections along the journey, but the team's extensive experience and diverse backgrounds make them uniquely prepared to handle such shifts. The team is heavily invested in understanding what works and what doesn't, allowing for swift adjustments during this critical phase. Ghiotti said, "I make a point of talking to our early customers every day. I ask them about what we can do better, what bugged them in the experience, explaining what we are fixing and why their feedback is so critical to us. We are customer obsessed." Still, one must bear in mind that the success of this venture to capture the young generation in Japan is not a foregone conclusion.

Ghiotti said, "One of the things I learned from my past experiences is that the recipe for success is very tricky to bottle. You can have the best idea, the most agile plans, a great team and still fail. I'm not trying to ascribe the best outcomes just to blind luck, but there is such a thing as being in the right place at the right time and no one knows that better than entrepreneurs. Our job as entrepreneurs is to create the most productive conditions for that magic to happen, and that, I think, is what makes the job of an entrepreneur uniquely exciting and fulfilling."

Foundations for The Future

- Invest in research to understand consumer behavior and needs, especially of the younger generation as the industry has largely failed to cater to this demographic.

- Keep a close eye on regulatory openings and make sure you understand their impact on the broader industry. A lot of financial innovation stems from regulatory opening and it can allow new players to enter a market.

- Don't underestimate the importance of local expertise. When entering a foreign market, it's crucial to onboard a team of local experts who can navigate local regulations and interpret customer insights.

III. MOVING FORWARD

It is my hope that the cases presented in this book have not only captivated you, but also sparked inspiration to tackle what's possible in the future of insurance. My intention was to offer insight into the unique attributes of the different countries discussed, illuminating the often distinct challenges faced by companies operating within these markets. Despite the diversity of the countries and organizations presented, which range from insurance incumbents and neo insurers to distribution-focused insurtechs, some fundamental lessons have emerged.

Each case presented in this book offers a treasure trove of valuable lessons that can benefit individuals embarking on new ventures or aiming to transform existing ones. Upon reviewing the entire set of case studies, a collection of resilient, shared lessons consistently surfaces which we will add as overarching Foundations for the Future:

1. Build a Customer-Focused Business
2. Embrace Change
3. Leverage the Power of Partnerships

Each of these key lessons will be examined in detail in this section. These guiding principles can act as a 'north star' and help insurers steering the course into the future of insurance amid the unpredictability of today's world.

12. Build a Customer-Focused Business

While we have been talking about becoming more customer centric in insurance for decades, only a few companies in this industry have successfully build a truly customer-focused business.

What does this term even mean?

A customer-focused business approach prioritizes the needs, preferences, and expectations of customers over those of the company. This approach involves seeing the business from the customer's perspective and shaping products, services, and the entire customer experience around what most effectively meets their needs.

Features of a customer-focused business include:

1. Personalization: Customer-focused businesses aim to tailor their products or services to match the individual needs and preferences of their customers.

2. Customer Experience: These businesses strive to offer a seamless, positive customer experience at every touchpoint. This could be in the buying experience, the user interface of a website or app or the interactions a customer has when getting service.

3. Feedback: Customer feedback is valued highly in these businesses. They actively seek, acknowledge, and use feedback to make improvements.

4. Relationship Building: A customer-focused business doesn't see each sale as a single transaction but instead seeks to build long-term relationships with its customers. This may involve loyalty programs, regular check-ins, personalized offers, etc.

The benefits of being a customer-focused business include increased customer satisfaction and loyalty; positive word of mouth; higher retention rates; and, ultimately, increased profits. It's a strategic approach that puts the customer at the center of any business decision, believing that happy, loyal customers lead to long-term business success.

Looking at the first feature of a customer-focused business, personalization, a prevalent issue the insurance industry is facing is the tendency of many incumbent insurers to favor a product-driven approach. In far too many instances, insurers design products grounded mainly in statistical data available to them, sidelining the actual needs of consumers. Similarly, existing products are often propelled into the market by agents and brokers without accounting for the evolving behavior or requirements of newer generations.

I do recognize the obstacles inherent in market research and focus groups regarding insurance products. Insurance, by its nature, is usually not the first thing consumers think about, making it challenging for insurers to pinpoint the real needs.

However, the case studies in this book are useful examples, showing how some innovative companies in Asia have cleverly created strategies to gently introduce insurance, especially to the younger generation. These strategies emphasize not just the importance of insurance, but also the benefits it offers in customers' day to day lives, fostering a deeper understanding and appreciation of the industry.

As we delve deeper, we find these Asian companies revolutionizing the traditional insurance paradigm through a blend of educational initiatives, targeted marketing, and nuanced product design. By harnessing the power of digital platforms, they are reaching out to the younger generation, demystifying the concept of insurance and highlighting its relevance in the context of their personal lives. They are not simply selling insurance; they are often fostering a culture of risk awareness.

Moreover, these companies are keenly aware that today's young customers demand more than just a product. They seek a holistic experience – one that is simple, transparent, and tailored to their unique needs. In response, these innovators have shifted their focus from mere product development to delivering personalized customer journeys. This shift marks a departure from traditional business models, transforming insurance from a begrudgingly purchased necessity into a valued and trusted service.

The case studies in this book offer insights for anyone wishing to move from a product-centric to a customer-centric approach, embracing personalized products and services. Some of the examples highlight how innovative market research utilizing digital tools enables those companies to develop innovative product designs that are highly personalized and focused on customer needs.

Take, for instance, Hong Kong's insurtech firm, YAS. Rather than initiating their process from a product-centric perspective, they center their strategy around the real-world worries of consumers. The startup employs an innovative market research approach, gathering data from social media, blogs, and forums to uncover emerging trends and consumer pain points. By thoroughly analyzing this data, they detected an uptick in interest in outdoor activities among consumers, accompanied by a heightened concern for safety.

Seizing this market opportunity, YAS designed specialized insurance products targeting hiking, biking, and other outdoor activities. Beyond that, they introduced a unique loyalty-as-insurance model. This concept cleverly aligns the offering with the customer's immediate context and mindset, prompting them to consider the crucial role of insurance in mitigating the risks they encounter in their current activities.

In essence, YAS not only identified existing consumer worries but also strategically engineered a sales funnel that captures customers at the right time. This is not only a great example of personalization but also of customer experience as it ensures that customers are engaged at an opportune moment when they are in the ideal frame of mind to appreciate the importance of insurance.

Identifying the right time to approach a consumer and raising awareness about the significance and advantages of insurance is particularly vital in countries grappling with low financial literacy. In such a landscape, Indonesian insurtech Qoala emphasizes the value of consumer education by favoring opt-out embedded insurance products over purely seeking higher conversion rates. In addition, their strategy echoes the practice of sampling a spoonful of ice cream before committing to a whole scoop, paying respect to the fact that many consumers are buying insurance for the first time.

And just like YAS, Qoala invests in research to pinpoint the dominant concerns of people, translating those concerns into personalized small ticket, micro insurance products. While these products may not yield high margins, they serve as an effective tool to showcase and educate consumers about the benefits of insurance.

Rather than launching with a complex product, Qoala employs a gradual approach to introduce consumers to financial products. This method builds the necessary trust for the subsequent introduction of more comprehensive insurance solutions.

While it's undeniable that these micro-premium, entry products won't significantly bolster any company's bottom line, they represent a crucial first step in customer acquisition and are a strategy to build long-term relationships with customers – another feature of customer-focused businesses.

Bolttech is another example of an insurtech that has understood the importance of building a strong relationship with customers. The company not only dedicates considerable efforts to identifying and crafting the right entry product but also strategizes for subsequent stages. They ponder the logical product progression for any insurance product as they are aware that there is no 'one-size-fits-all' solution and personalization is key. To understand what customers want, bolttech not only conducts market research before launching a product but collects customer feedback on a regular basis with a structured approach.

Being able to collect customer feedback first-hand is something that OneDegree also values very highly and is in fact another important feature of a customer-focused business. OneDegree constantly speaks to their customers to understand how they can improve their products and services. Being directly engaged with customers and receiving their feedback forces the team to learn and grow. Leung explicitly stressed the importance of engaging in the B2C sector and talking directly to customers as he believes it is imperative to fostering innovation.

Ghiotti follows a similar strategy. When she launched Habitto in June 2023, she shared, "I make a point of talking to our early customers every day. I ask them about what we can do better, what bugged them in the experience, explaining what we are fixing and why their feedback is so critical to us. We are customer obsessed."

Collecting feedback is not only important to understand how satisfied customers are with a product but also to identify obstacles customers might experience in their user journey, an often-overlooked component of the overall customer experience.

Tune Protect has a strong focus on optimizing their customer experience by simplifying their processes. The goal of their Three-Three-Three philosophy is to increase transparency for their customers. Within three minutes, consumers can buy a policy; within three hours, they will hear back regarding an enquiry; and within three days, Tune Protect will pay out their claim. This way, the company was able to turn its initially negative NPS positive, from -16% to +14% within nine months.

Today, NPS is a common KPI that can be used to understand how customer-focused an organization is. Ping An had already introduced this KPI in 2000 and was the first insurer to do so in China. It was part of the company's transition from a product-driven strategy to a customer-focused strategy, being considered a trailblazer at that time.

In India, PhonePe undertook extensive efforts, delving into insurance regulations in great detail, to create a customer experience and user journey that allows people with limited financial literacy to buy insurance products online. As industry insiders would confirm, insurance is rarely a pull-product. Thus, it's a significant accomplishment that PhonePe managed to digitally sell to individuals who have never purchased an insurance product before.

Achieving this feat was possible only with the right product, coupled with a user journey that removes all jargon and complexity. By understanding what customers are looking for and what obstacles keep them from buying insurance online, PhonePe succeeded in adding insurance offerings to a digital payment platform.

I believe everyone agrees that customer-focus is important but building a customer-focused business is unfortunately not as straightforward. The stark reality is that we frequently find ourselves trapped in our daily routines, challenges and constraints. During my tenure as a management consultant, I worked on a project with one of the leading global insurers. Our mission was to implement the core system used in the home country at an overseas branch together with a new user interface.

The entire team was stretched thin, project costs had skyrocketed, and every participant was primarily focused on getting the system to run while maintaining compliance with local regulations. Amid such a fast-paced project, there was neither the mental bandwidth to analyze customer needs nor leftover budget to conduct research or focus groups.

This scenario, while unfortunate, is not uncommon.

A significant portion of the business that is unrelated to enhancing customer experience, often ends up consuming the lion's share of resources. This results in a minimal allocation left for areas that could directly improve a customer's journey and satisfaction. However, in an ideal world, every aspect would begin with the customer. Achieving this shift necessitates a change in mindset more than anything else.

Amazon serves as a prime example of a company built on an unwavering dedication to customer focus while maintaining a high level of efficiency and automation to reduce costs. From its earliest days, the company has followed a customer-centric philosophy, with its founder, Jeff Bezos, coining the phrase 'customer obsession'.

Amazon constantly strives to understand its customers' needs, aspirations, and pain points, using this understanding to shape its services and products. Whether it's the convenience of one-click ordering, personalized recommendations, or the ability to return products with minimal hassle, Amazon continuously refines its operations to improve the customer experience.

> *"If you look at the financial services industry, they are missing empathy ... whereas tech giants are really good at this."*
>
> *– Andy Ann*
> *Co-Founder, YAS*

YAS's Andy Ann reflected on the contrast between Amazon and our industry. He said, "If you look at the financial services industry, they are missing empathy. They do not have an understanding of the customer experience, the customer journey, the user experience and user interface, whereas tech giants are really good at this. Amazon knows us inside and out, they have AI recommendations, and the user experience is seamless."

Even in their pursuit of new innovations, like venturing into drone deliveries or establishing cashier-less stores, the driving factor remains the desire to enhance the customer journey. This relentless customer focus has been instrumental in Amazon's rise to become one of the world's most valuable companies.

13. Embrace Change

It might be the risk adverse nature of insurance, or the strict regulatory environment in which we operate, but many in the industry find it challenging to adopt an agile style of work. What I kept hearing during my interviews for this book or when talking to insurtech startups for the podcasts I run, was that insurance incumbents aren't fast enough to react to market changes. While the insurance industry is crucial to a country's economy and requires a careful approach, organizations should also foster the ability to respond swiftly to an increasingly dynamic world and view change as an ally rather than an adversary.

The relentless pace of technological advancement, shifting regulatory landscapes, evolving customer expectations, and unpredictable risk scenarios necessitate that insurers adopt a more flexible, iterative approach to their strategic planning and operational models. Traditional practices that may have once proven successful may no longer yield the desired outcomes in this ever-changing environment. Adopting an iterative approach enables insurers to constantly test and refine their offerings and processes, incorporate feedback, and learn in real time, thereby driving constant improvement.

It's time for the insurance industry to not just adapt to change, but to confidently own it and embed it within their strategic toolkit.

While fundamental shifts in business strategy or model are mostly relevant for startups, the ability to pivot when circumstances demand and recalibrate swiftly and effectively is important for companies at any size. A strategy change shouldn't be viewed as a shortcoming, but rather a valuable learning opportunity that allows the business to get even better. Both iteration and pivoting fortify an insurer's resilience, fostering their ability to innovate, keep pace with emerging trends, and ultimately deliver superior value to their stakeholders. Embracing change, rather than resisting it, can be a defining feature of successful insurers in this rapidly evolving landscape.

In the previous lesson about the importance of building a customer-focused business, we looked at product development and the need to conduct extensive market research to understand customer needs. While most companies conduct market research before launching a new product, many only analyze static data sets instead of new, real time data. However, only taking historic, mostly static data sets into account isn't good enough anymore. Just think about the recent COVID-19 pandemic that turned many aspects of daily life upside-down. Even for classic products like motor or life insurance, the rich historical data available could not reflect the situation the world found itself in.

However, it doesn't take a global pandemic to understand the importance of real-time data. To design products that meet the needs of the next generation and take technological advancements as well as changes in behavior into account, insurers need to start using new and dynamic data sources that help them understand the real world dynamics. Creating a better understanding of the current situation and how it's developing can set you up to better embrace change because you see the need for it coming.

In Indonesia, Qoala analyzed the traffic in Jakarta for months to collect enough data points to build an initial version of their flight delay insurance coverage. YAS and OneDegree analyzed data from social media platforms and blogs to identify what consumers were looking for.

However, this is just the first step in developing a new product. The next, though equally important step is to collect direct and indirect customer feedback and make changes, if the data suggests to do so. Only once a product is live will companies know for sure what works and what doesn't. "If you ask me which product will succeed and which one will fail at launch, I will tell you I actually have no clue!" Shared Tune Protect CEO, Nambiar.

Bolttech shared a similar experience. In 2020, the insurtech launched a COVID-19 coverage in partnership with a telecommunication partner, intending to cross-sell it to existing customers. Market research suggested that COVID-19 was a prevalent concern, leading bolttech to predict the product would fly off the digital shelves. However, sales fell short of expectations, prompting bolttech to substitute it with a more relevant and contextual offering.

Bolttech, OneDegree, Qoala and Tune Protect all reported that they make regular tweaks once a product is live, considering this change part of the product development process and not a failure in their initial market research. That is, they build the expectation of change into their go-to-market strategy right from the start. This also allows the companies to launch products faster as they do not need to be super confident that any given product is priced or structured perfectly at launch or any time after that. Having the ability to monitor a product real-time allows them to make daily tweaks until they reach a level that promises profitability and meets customer needs. And if conditions change, the product can change with them to stay relevant and financially viable.

In fact, one of the reasons OneDegree decided to launch a licensed insurer was to be able to control product design and have the autonomy to experiment with products. OneDegree's Leung said, "We really wanted to own the product and have control of all decisions on the product itself. And it has proven to really be a key value for us as an organization. How we can be so fast in iterating and changing our product and ensuring product-market fit is because we control what we do on underwriting criteria, on the pricing, on the design of product, etc. Therefore, decision making is a lot faster."

> "...because we control what we do on underwriting criteria, on the pricing, on the design of product, etc. Therefore, decision making is a lot faster.."
>
> – Alex Leung
> Co-founder,
> OneDegree

Being a licensed, full-stack insurer allows OneDegree to embrace change and pivot where they think necessary. And it is not only about the algorithm but also about product features. Being able to quickly make changes to a product so it is more attractive to customers is especially important when selling digitally as no sales force is there to push the product into the market.

I acknowledge that launching a new and innovative product that uses new data sources can be problematic or difficult as regulators in different markets may be very strict around approving rate plans or tariffs.

This is especially the case when it comes to life or health insurance products – and for good reason. It is the responsibility of the regulators to ensure a product is calculated responsibly. To manage this without stifling innovation or progress, many regulators have launched regulatory sandboxes that allow insurers and insurtechs to experiment with new product designs and embrace change while ensuring the stability of the industry.

However, this lesson goes beyond just designing products and using real-time data to enhance them. It's about constantly tracking if your actions yield the expected results, and if not, learning to adjust your strategy accordingly and embrace change in all parts of the organization, even on a strategic level.

In Japan, Habitto discovered that financial institutions have failed to sufficiently cater to the younger generation. The existing sales channels and ways products are marketed often do not appeal to this customer base. Many insurers in Japan are confronted with a scenario where their traditional target customers are rapidly aging and gradually disappearing, yet many have not made the necessary adjustments to attract a new, younger customer segment. This lack of adaptability is now creating a significant opportunity for insurtechs like Habitto to gain a foothold in a highly mature market.

Startups, in contrast to traditional insurance incumbents, frequently cultivate a culture that welcomes change, including at the strategic level. After all, it is what keeps them ahead of the curve, allowing them to seize new opportunities, tackle challenges proactively, and continuously learn and improve.

Pivoting is a strategic maneuver startups often undertake when they recognize their current business model or product isn't meeting market needs or achieving desired results. In this process, companies make a fundamental change to their strategy. This can result in the startup discovering a more successful trajectory, leading to growth and sustainability in the long run.

Take PhonePe, for instance. The company had established their go-to-market strategy as an insurance agent. However, their research indicated a need for adjustments to better capitalize on the market opportunity. Through their research, they discovered that customers felt a lack of choice. Identifying this gap, PhonePe transformed into a licensed insurance broker, enabling them to offer products from any insurance provider on their platform.

Likewise, bolttech, despite initially acquiring underwriting licenses in Hong Kong and Thailand, the insurtech saw greater potential in operating as a balance sheet light company focusing on distribution of embedded insurance products. As a result, they sold their local unit in Thailand to Thai insurtech Roojai in July 2023.[62] This move underscores bolttech's willingness to revisit and revise previous decisions that may no longer align with their strategic vision or the evolution of the environment they're operating in, exemplifying their commitment to adaptability and change.

Change is a constant and inevitable part of life for organizations of any size. Being able to embrace this change is arguably what transformed Ping An into a leading financial services conglomerate globally. The company navigated through four significant strategic transformations to reach this milestone.

In the first phase, Ping An laid solid foundations, acquiring essential licenses and developing the knowledge and skills to manage a diverse insurance business.

They then switched from a product-centric to a customer-centric strategy, which included integrating their client database for a comprehensive customer view.

The introduction of smartphones and rise of Chinese tech giants like Baidu, Alibaba, and Tencent spurred another significant shift in Ping An's strategy. Founder Peter Ma foresaw the immense potential of the digitization of the financial services industry. This insight sparked Ping An's evolution into a tech-first company, transitioning its entire operation to the cloud between 2010 and 2016, a feat few financial institutions of this size have achieved even today.

A few years later, Ping An pivoted again to its famous ecosystem strategy and the goal to become a world-leading integrated finance and healthcare services provider.

I believe we can all agree that embracing change may be beneficial. However, it is often human nature to resist change and actively seek justifications to maintain the *status quo*. Resistance to change often stems from cognitive biases, notably confirmation bias and *status quo* bias. These biases drive individuals to actively seek information that aligns with their existing beliefs.

---

[62] Sri, Deepti, "Thai insurtech firm Roojai buys local unit of Bolttech biz," *Tech In Asia*, 5 July 2023.

Nambiar from Tune Protect shared his approach to overcome our natural resistance to change. He organizes a strategy meeting every two months involving 30 employees from various parts of the organization. Everyone proposes ideas and, importantly, no criticism is allowed at the outset. By not focusing on potential hurdles or difficulties in implementing these ideas initially, the team can freely visualize the real-world impact of these ideas. This approach fosters a culture of creativity and innovation, encouraging change rather than shying away from it.

At the beginning of this book, I talked about Everett Rogers' Diffusion of Innovations theory. The theory, as discussed earlier, explains how ideas and technologies spread through societies. It identifies five stages of the diffusion process: knowledge, persuasion, decision, implementation, and confirmation. It then categorizes individuals into five categories: innovators, early adopters, early majority, late majority, and laggards.

When applied to the insurance industry, this theory offers us insights into why some insurance incumbents might struggle with implementing an agile work style or swiftly responding to the market. Most likely, they fall into the late majority or laggard categories of the adopter continuum, hesitant to embrace change until they are sure of its effectiveness and profitability. In contrast, insurtech startups, often innovators and early adopters, are more willing to take risks and pioneer new approaches.

Being in one category or another does not mean you can or cannot embrace change, though. It just means you need to be aware of the inherent, internal resistance to change we all face so you can navigate through it. That means any company – legacy or startup – can embrace change. Some may just be better positioned than others to do so.

In today's fast developing world, the insurance industry must embrace change on the operational level as well as on a strategic level. The traditional approach of meticulous planning and methodical execution that has served the industry well in the past is now being challenged by a rapidly evolving market and customer landscape. Companies presented in this book are leading the way in illustrating how to successfully navigate this new paradigm, by embracing an iterative and agile approach, making smart strategic pivots, and capitalizing on the power of real-time data to make decisions.

The new mantra for success in this evolving scenario seems to be: launch, learn, iterate, and pivot if necessary. Staying nimble and adaptable is the key. This approach expedites decision-making processes and fosters a culture of ongoing learning and enhancement. In essence, it's about owning the change, making it a part of the organization's DNA, thereby ensuring continuous growth and development in an ever-evolving industry landscape.

14. Leverage the Power of Partnerships

Another common theme that has emerged through the various case studies is the undeniable truth that no entity, regardless of its size or tenure in the business, can chart the future solo. Insurance firms that foster strategic partnerships will have an edge, enabling a new paradigm of risk management, service delivery, and value creation.

The future of insurance is not a single entity but rather an ecosystem of diverse players, including legacy and startup insurers, technology companies, data providers, alternative distribution channels, regulators, and customers. Insurers and insurtechs that acknowledge this interwoven tapestry and proactively seek collaboration with partners will reap the benefits of synergies and groundbreaking innovations that simply wouldn't be possible in a siloed approach.

The rise of digital platforms and marketplaces has opened up new ways to reach consumers. Both, PhonePe and Habitto have understood the power of alternative distribution channels with a mobile-first strategy and are leveraging partnerships with insurers as a source for considerable revenue. Many insurers face challenges when trying to develop new distribution channels, but, truthfully, there's no necessity for them to build these platforms independently. Super apps like PhonePe or startups like Habitto are often better equipped to build such channels. PhonePe's strong customer-focus enabled the fintech to successfully establish a pull-channel for insurance products within their app creating a win-win situation for the company and their insurance partners.

While it is too early to tell if Habitto will succeed at attracting the younger generation in Japan with their mobile-first approach, their overall strategy heavily depends on identifying the right partners that are willing to integrate with them. The fact that they were able to confirm their first partners and go live within a few months is a sign that insurers have understood the power of such partnerships and the opportunities these new distribution channels present.

In this new world of partnerships, insurers have the chance to collaborate with a multitude of new distribution platforms, offering their products directly to consumers. While the examples of PhonePe and Habitto are centered around financial products, new embedded insurance solutions also allow for strategic partnerships outside of financial services.

By weaving insurance solutions into non-insurance goods or services, partners enable point-of-sale insurance purchases for consumers, thereby making the process effortless and user-friendly. Such integration is inherently partnership-dependent, as insurers need to collaborate with businesses outside their traditional domain, which often requires a mindset shift.

> *"Whether you're buying bite-sized travel insurance or motor insurance ... the brand doesn't matter as much because ... your trust is more with the original brand ... and not the insurance provider partnering with that brand.."*
>
> – Rohit Nambiar
> Group CEO,
> Tune Protect

In the context of such embedded insurance partnerships, the insurer's role is often less prominent, operating more in the background than as a central figure. Here, insurance is subtly integrated into a range of offerings, rather than being the focal point of the transaction. This isn't an "ego-system" revolving around the insurer's stature but an "ecosystem" where diverse partners unite to work harmoniously towards a common goal.

In this ecosystem, roles are not rigid but fluid, based on the strengths of the partners. If a partner is a strong consumer brand and excels in client interaction and engagement, it makes sense for the insurer to relinquish the front stage, recede into the background, and support the customer-facing processes. This ensures the best use of each entity's core competencies, enhancing the overall effectiveness and success of the partnership.

Tune Protect's Nambiar shared, "Whether you're buying bite-sized travel insurance or motor insurance, which is a highly commoditized product, the brand doesn't matter as much because you're buying it from someone you trust, and you have the belief that they have an insurance partner who will deliver. Your trust is more with the original brand you associated yourself with and not the insurance provider partnering with that brand."

In other words, the trust is placed more in the original brand than in the insurance provider. In this way, any insurer, small or large, can successfully leverage these established relationships as an alternative distribution channel for their products. By partnering with trusted brands, they can increase their market reach and effectively drive product uptake without having to build or own the channel.

Bolttech is another example of a prominent global player in this context. The company's business model is centered around establishing strategic partnerships between insurers and non-insurance brands in telecommunications, financial services, e-commerce, and super apps, with the goal to explore and develop new distribution channels. As of May 2023, bolttech's insurance exchange connects more than 230 insurance providers with over 700 distribution partners offline and online.

Bolttech echoed Tune Protect's insight - when integrating insurance solutions into a strong consumer brand's ecosystem there is often no need or value to promote the brand of the insurance partner.

Those embedded insurance solutions aren't new but what has changed the game in recent years and accelerated the growth of such partnerships is the online integration with digital marketplaces through open APIs. APIs allow insurers to easily and cost-effectively integrate their systems with partners, supporting real-time sharing of data and functionalities. In essence, this is the technology enabling partnerships in the modern marketplace.

Most companies discussed in this book, if not all, harness the power of APIs for seamless integration with partners. This capability of offering API integration was a decisive factor in the initial success of YAS in coming to market. It allowed the insurtech to integrate with payment platform Octopus, bus company KMB and connect it all to their insurance partner Generali. And it was a critical differentiator between YAS and their incumbent competitor that allowed them to win the deal in the first place.

API capabilities is also what allowed Qoala to integrate micro insurance solutions with digital ecosystems like ride hailing app Grab. Without the partnership with those digital ecosystems and the cost effective integration via API, the insurtech wouldn't be able to follow their strategy of offering bite-sized insurance solutions as a means to increase financial literacy and educate consumers about the benefits of insurance.

However, the focus isn't solely on digital ecosystems. Partnerships with physical, brick-and-mortar stores also aid companies in reaching their customers and enhancing their services. Bolttech, despite its strong focus on digital, is working with partners that run physical stores and so is pet insurance provider OneDegree. The Hong Kong-based insurer formed an alliance with veterinarian clinics, pet shop brands and NGOs, although with a different strategy compared to bolttech.

In the case of OneDegree, those partnerships are part of an affiliate marketing strategy to reach new customers and build a strong brand reputation in this segment. As the holder of a virtual insurance license, OneDegree isn't allowed to leverage any other direct distribution channel but their own D2C channel. However, the mentioned partnerships have helped the neo insurer tremendously to build their brand and have been a strategic component of their initial business plan when they first applied for the virtual insurance license with the insurance regulator in Hong Kong. Those partnerships were what made selling insurance D2C feasible for a newcomer brand.

However, partnerships can be leveraged beyond distribution channels and affiliate marketing. A company that has truly understood the power of partnerships is Ping An.

Ping An's ecosystem strategy is an excellent example of how to create synergy between various sectors and services. Rather than operating as a standalone insurance company, Ping An has created a vast ecosystem that spans across healthcare, automobile services, real estate, and financial services. This interconnected network of services enables Ping An to leverage cross-sectoral data, gather insights, and drive innovation. Their partnership approach includes internal collaboration across various units, collaboration with external partners, as well as leveraging their Global Voyager Fund to connect companies, they have strategically invested in, with their extensive global network of businesses and associates.

The case of Snapsheet's partnership with Ping An offers a profound demonstration of the power of strategic partnerships. The claims management platform has been in the US market for a few years but was lacking a visual claims analysis module. This gap was addressed when Ping An came on board as an investor. Ping An's technological competence, especially with visual claims analysis, filled the gap within Snapsheet's product offering, enhancing the overall value proposition of the platform.

The successful integration of Ping An's technology into Snapsheet's platform underlines the potential of leveraging partner strengths to deliver better services and access new markets. If Ping An had decided to introduce this technology independently in the US, it would have faced formidable barriers. However, through its calculated investment in Snapsheet, Ping An found a swift and effective entry route to seven of the top 10 US auto insurers, a testament to the power of strategic partnerships.

In addition, this partnership holds the potential to enhance Ping An's visual claims technology by feeding it with more data. Most AI models improve with larger data sets, making them more accurate. Deploying the model in a different country might also help in getting access to large enough data sets for motor vehicles that are not as common in China, training the model on more variety.

Ping An's move not only illustrates the company's tech-centered philosophy but also its commitment to fostering innovation and growth through strategic partnerships. Contrary to some insurers who guard their innovations from competitors, this example highlights how broadening access to technology through collaborations can yield greater business success, thereby underlining the benefits of a more open, partnership-driven approach.

In China, Ping An's ecosystem of internet companies significantly bolsters their insurance and financial services business, while globally, they have made strategic forays into the software-as-a-service (SaaS) market. It also underscores Ping An's stature as not merely a retail financial services group, but a technology company that actively engages in importing and exporting technological innovation.

Within only four decades, Ping An has grown to be one of the largest insurers globally and many believe their unique ecosystem approach is one of the success factors.

In conclusion, the future of insurance hinges on an interconnected ecosystem, rather than standalone entities operating in a closed manner. Partnerships and alliances will be vital for insurers to innovate, create value, and reach new customers. The solitary insurer concept is yielding to a dynamic model where roles and responsibilities are flexible and collective strengths contribute to shared success. This transformation, extending beyond structure to mindset, demands a holistic approach. Insurers and insurtechs must view themselves as vital yet interconnected parts of a larger framework, rather than independent entities. This shift, coupled with effective collaboration, is crucial for navigating the future insurance landscape successfully.

15. Evolving Ahead

The insurance industry, like many other sectors, has undergone profound changes as a result of technological innovation. New risks have emerged, and insurers have had to adapt their offerings to cover these. At the same time, technology has provided a wealth of tools and approaches for insurers to better understand, manage, and mitigate risks.

In the midst of this evolution, it is important that we step back and reflect on what these developments mean for our society at large. As we continue to digitize and harness the power of data and AI, it's time to ask critical questions. Are we employing these new technologies and methodologies as a force for good, for the betterment of all customers? Or are we risking their misuse for discriminatory practices and enabling adverse selection?

Profit maximization is a universal goal for organizations, be it publicly listed companies accountable to their shareholders, or insurtech startups striving to generate revenue for survival. However, this pursuit should not overshadow the broader societal role that insurance plays. It might, therefore, fall upon regulatory bodies to ensure that the industry stays on track and continues to serve as a critical economic pillar.

For the broader economic health of any country, it's crucial that insurance is accessible and affordable, enabling people and companies to effectively manage their risks.

Changes in societal demographics but also geopolitical conflicts and the climate crisis are putting insurance providers at the heart of the solution, challenging them to devise products and services that meet these changing needs without compromising on accessibility and affordability. An insurance sector that can meet these demands will not only ensure the wellbeing of individuals and companies, but also contribute to the stability and resilience of the economy at large.

Emerging technologies like advanced data analytics and AI can be instrumental in enhancing accessibility and personalization of insurance. By identifying unconventional distribution channels and facilitating the integration of insurance into everyday life, these technologies can bridge the gap between insurers and consumers and make insurance protection a more intuitive part of people's lives. Simultaneously, they can offer better risk understanding and management, enabling insurance providers to more accurately assess and evaluate risks.

However, this should not only lead to competitive advantages and the ability to identify unfavorable risk profiles. Instead, I envision an industry that plays a more proactive role in people's lives. Rather than being a mere safety net activated when adversity strikes, insurance can evolve into a comprehensive package of products and services that holistically addresses risk.

Through partnerships and the power of predictive analytics, insurers can help individuals anticipate potential risks and take preventive measures. Tools and resources can be provided to help customers manage the risks they face, promoting a more proactive approach to risk management. And, when preventive measures fall short, insurance will, of course, remain the financial backstop, cushioning the financial blow of unexpected events.

In essence, this represents a shift from insurance as a product to insurance as a service, one that spans the entire risk management spectrum, providing support and guidance at every step. It's a transformation that can enhance the value of insurance in people's lives, fostering a closer, more meaningful relationship between insurers and their customers. This, in turn, can contribute to greater resilience at both the individual and societal level, and ultimately, to a more secure future for all.

This shift, from viewing insurance as a product to embracing it as a comprehensive service signifies a profound change in the industry's perspective. Rather than offering a one-off product, insurance is now seen as a holistic process. It incorporates a spectrum of risk management strategies that guide and support customers throughout their journeys. This transformation has the potential to amplify the inherent value of insurance, embedding it more deeply into people's daily lives.

The new insurance as a service model fosters a more intimate, meaningful relationship between insurers and their customers. Instead of a purely transactional relationship based on purchasing a product, the interaction becomes ongoing and consultative. Insurers assist customers in identifying, understanding, and managing risks, which in turn promotes trust and customer loyalty. This deeper relationship not only ensures that the coverage is personalized and truly addresses customers' needs but also enables insurers to anticipate and adapt to changes in those needs over time.

Moreover, this transformative shift can lead to increased resilience at multiple levels. On an individual scale, consumers equipped with personalized risk management strategies are more prepared to face uncertainties. They become more resilient to potential shocks, knowing they are adequately insured and have a trusted advisor to guide them. At the societal level, when more people are insured and better prepared for risks, it enhances the collective resilience against widespread crises, from natural disasters to economic downturns.

This insurance transformation, in effect, paves the way towards a future where everyone is better prepared for uncertainty. It encourages a more proactive, preventive approach to risk management. It underscores the role of insurance not just as a financial safety net, but as an integral part of people's lives that empowers them to face the future with confidence. By leveraging this shift, insurers can play a critical role in shaping a more secure future for all.

As Lunani stated, "I don't think there's any country which has become a great economy without being well insured, because there's going to be bumps in the road. And if your economy and your people are well protected, they will be able to get through the difficult patches and achieve something greater because insurance enables them to take risks."

Throughout my life, I've frequently encountered individuals who hold a negative view towards insurance, considering it a necessary evil. I envision a future where the significance of insurance for a nation's overall prosperity is widely recognized. Concurrently, I hope we, working in insurance, will embrace our responsibility and construct products and services that contribute to a sustainable future for everyone.

ACKNOWLEDGMENTS

I am deeply grateful to the many people who supported this book directly and indirectly. I would like to start by thanking each of the people from the companies featured here who willingly gave hours of their time for interviews. By sharing their experiences, they helped breathe life into the case studies and enriched them with valuable lessons for everyone. A special thank you to Andy Ann from YAS; Alex Leung from OneDegree; Harshet Lunani from Qoala; Rob Schimek and Melissa Wong from bolttech; Hemant Gala from PhonePe; Jonathan Larsen from Ping An; Rohit Nambiar from Tune Protect; and Sam Ghiotti from Habitto.

In addition, several more people from these great companies generously gave me their time and effort to make this all happen, and deserve a public thanking. Kate Geraghty from bolttech coordinated everything, sat through most of the interviews, and provided loads of additional information. Harinee Sivaprakasam from PhonePe coordinated my requests and helped to keep things moving. Gareth Hewett and Maria Ma (马金晓) from Ping An coordinated all the conversations, helped getting the required approvals, and shared additional info so I could accurately tell Ping An's story. Rozieana Binti Jamaluddin at Tune Protect has been so helpful to me for many months, coordinating everything needed to finalize the chapter. Thank you all so much, I literally could not have done this without all of you.

Another thank you to the many people who helped make these cases come together by opening doors and providing introductions to the founders of these companies. Thanks to others who contributed, helped, guided along the way, or supported the project.

Similarly, there are people who gave their time and support to bring their company into this book, but ultimately things didn't work out. That's the nature of doing work like this. Sometimes, circumstances make it hard to share your story at a given time, but what they gave of themselves in the hopes of being able to do that is still greatly appreciated. Maybe they'll be able to share their story next time.

There was also an army of supporters of this work that are too numerous to name individually, but some warrant a special shout out for truly going above and beyond. My husband, Tyson Nicholas, who aways has my back and tries really hard to share my excitement for the insurance industry. Michael Waitze, whom I am running the Asia InsurTech Podcast and InsurTech Amplified with. Without the network we have built together over the years, this wouldn't have been possible. Michael's unwavering support, particularly during the recording of the audio book, has been instrumental.

And how could I ever forget Bryan Falchuk. Bryan's guidance has been the compass by which I navigated the intricate journey of writing this book. His feedback, both insightful and relentless, sculpted every page and chapter into its final form. The hours he dedicated, the expertise he shared, and the unwavering support he provided have been the cornerstones of this endeavor. This book, in many ways, stands as a testament to our collective efforts and Bryan's profound influence. Thank you Bryan for being more than just an advisor; you've been a mentor and a driving force behind this work.

And last but not least, I would like to thank you, the Esteemed Readers. A book breathes life not just from the ink and paper it's crafted upon, but from the eyes that peruse its pages and the minds that absorb its essence. To each one of you who has taken the time to journey through these chapters, thank you. Your curiosity, engagement, and the willingness to immerse yourself in this work have given it true purpose and meaning. May the insights you've gained not only enhance your personal life but also propel your career and contribute to the advancement of your organization. Here's to every thought provoked, emotion stirred, and conversation sparked. Your readership is deeply cherished, and I am profoundly grateful for your time and trust.

ABOUT THE AUTHOR

Theresa Blissing is a seasoned insurance professional with a strong background in operational roles with insurers, innovation consulting and academic research. Born into an insurance family, her insurance career officially began in 2004 when she joined Italian insurer Generali in Frankfurt, Germany. She held various roles within the company, including an international stint in Hong Kong.

In 2015, Theresa left Generali. Fascinated by the potential of new technologies and their impact on the insurance industry, she decided to delve into a new challenge and pursue a master's program with a research component, focusing her study on the adoption of big data in the Southeast Asian insurance industry. The research was an industry-first and was published in a paper that she presented at the International Conference on Business, Big-Data, and Decision Sciences (ICBBD).

Theresa then transitioned her career to management consulting. She worked with a range of consulting firms and started her own consulting and research practice. With her expertise in InsurTech and innovation, she collaborated with startups, startup accelerators, and venture builders. Theresa also continued to engage with the world of academia and was teaching at the Bangkok School of Management and serving as a guest lecturer at the Singapore College of Insurance and Chulalongkorn University.

In 2019, Theresa co-founded the Asia InsurTech Podcast to bring Asia's insurance success stories to a global audience. As of 2023, the podcast is one of the largest InsurTech podcasts globally with listeners in over 160 countries.

Theresa continues to push the boundaries of insurance innovation. She has relocated to New York City in 2023 and is working as an independent consultant. Together with Michael Waitze she has also launched a new global podcast – InsurTech Amplified.

Subscribe to Our Insurance Podcasts
asiainsurtechpodcast.com
insurtechamplified.com
future-of-insurance.com/podcast

Connect with Theresa Blissing
theresablissing.com
LinkedIn: linkedin.com/in/theresablissing

Get Updates on The FOI Series
future-of-insurance.com/updates

Other Books in The Future of Insurance Series
The Future of Insurance: From Disruption to Evolution, Volume I. The Incumbents
The Future of Insurance: From Disruption to Evolution, Volume II. The Startups
The Future of Insurance: From Disruption to Evolution, Volume III. The Collaborators

Made in the USA
Middletown, DE
14 October 2023

40613352R00106